IRAQ, VIETNAM, AND
THE LIMITS OF AMERICAN POWER

IRAQ, VIETNAM,

AND THE LIMITS

OF AMERICAN POWER

———

Robert K. Brigham

PublicAffairs • New York

Published in the United States by PublicAffairs™,
a member of the Perseus Books Group.

Designed by Mark McGarry, Texas Type & Bookworks
Text set in Dante

A CIP catalog record for this book is available from the Library of Congress
ISBN-13: 978-1-58648-499-6
First Edition
10 9 8 7 6 5 4 3 2 1

For my daughter,
Taylor Church Brigham

CONTENTS

PREFACE

After five years of conflict, the war in Iraq is not another Vietnam. It is far worse. Having the experience and lessons of Vietnam as a guide, the Bush administration charged headlong into a protracted war with little regard for history or the limits of U.S. power.

The first edition of this book raised the question of whether Iraq would turn into a war with the corrosive characteristics of Vietnam. That is no longer the issue. The Iraq War has created an array of new problems, and the United States will be coping with them for a generation, just as it had to struggle with the consequences of Vietnam. In this book, I argue that the Bush administration, in fighting a war of choice, has limited future U.S. foreign policy options, a limit that will have disastrous consequences. Americans may turn inward following the Iraq War, fearing that engagement with the outside world might lead to another protracted conflict with limited results. There will likely be an Iraq syndrome that matches the self-imposed foreign-policy restrictions and national malaise that followed Vietnam.

Hearing echoes of Vietnam, the United States refused to intervene to stop genocide in Cambodia, the Balkans, and Rwanda before it was too late for hundreds of thousands of innocent people. The great tragedy of the Iraq War is that foreign policy blunders there may limit U.S. military action where it may be required later.

Furthermore, the United States has set back its Middle East agenda considerably. Once seen as an honest broker in the Middle East, the United States under the Bush administration has squandered its power and reputation in the region by mishandling the war and regional diplomacy. Whatever gains the United States made in the Middle East during the 1970s, 1980s, and 1990s were quickly washed away by a misguided policy based on naive assumptions about the role of the United States in the world and its ability to promote change through military power alone. The recent military surge in Iraq has produced some victories and increased security in some places, but it has not had much impact on the Baghdad government. Prime Minister Jawad al-Maliki has not created the kind of legitimate political institutions necessary to guarantee a civil society inside Iraq. Baghdad has simply focused too much on security issues and not enough on political legitimacy and institution building. Furthermore, the White House has refused to build the architecture necessary to find a political solution through the construction of a government of reconciliation and concord. Exacerbating this problem has been the Bush administration's outright rejection of a role for the United Nations.

There will also be a domestic price for choosing war in Iraq. Paying for the war will be a burden on the country and its taxpayers for a decade. The U.S. economy has been in a tailspin for much of the war, following years of unprecedented economic growth, proving the old adage that it is difficult to have both guns and butter. Huge budget deficits and the price tag of trillions of dollars for the war in Iraq during the Bush years will require fiscal restraint and sacrifice in the near future. The United States now faces an economic recession fueled in part by the war in Iraq. In addition, domestic politics have become even more partisan and divisive. Democrats in Congress and Republicans in the White House have failed to act on the mandate for change in Iraq given to them by American voters in the 2006 midterm elections. Voters now want to move beyond this partisanship and overwhelmingly favor an end to the Iraq War.

Even after five years of conflict, it is quite likely that the end of the Iraq War will combine an escalation of violence with a negotiated U.S. withdrawal that leaves the major political questions of the war unresolved. The end result may be a bloody civil war in Iraq with regional and international consequences. Rather than spreading democracy throughout the region, the United States has, in fact, introduced greater instability with increased political and military pressure on America's Middle Eastern allies. And America's enemies will be emboldened, not because of U.S. military weakness, but because of recklessness in Washington. The progressive impulse in American foreign policy has led to the realization in some circles that there generally is no political corollary to American military strength when the United States engages in nation building abroad.

The lesson Iraq teaches us, then, if we care to listen, is that the United States should not use its overwhelming power arbitrarily. A mature nation, a nation with a proper sense of its own history and power, does not engage in wars of choice. It is now time for the

United States to reorient its power in the Middle East and to engage the world as a superpower with a clear sense of its mission. The first step is to create a framework for successful statecraft. For eight years the Bush administration has refused the diplomatic path in the Middle East. Now is the time to reverse that decision. It will take a decade for the United States to reestablish its power and prestige, but with bold leadership, such change is possible.

CHAPTER ONE

AMERICA GOES TO WAR

PRESIDENT GEORGE W. Bush took the United States to war in Iraq with soaring rhetoric about American ideals and deep-seated fears about security. He used heightened threat perceptions created by the horrific events of September 11, 2001, to make war against Saddam Hussein's Iraq and a global terrorist network a necessity. By linking Saddam's brutal rule with international terrorism—a connection that did not exist—the president was making the case for a preemptive strike against Iraq. The Bush administration convinced a majority of the American people and Congress that the United States would be more secure with a preventive strike against Baghdad. Furthermore, President Bush argued that the absence of democracy in the Middle East had given rise to terrorism and that it was his responsibility to change the course of history by using American power to overwhelm a tyrant who had aided and abetted the enemies of freedom.

The Bush White House believed that the world would support his decision to strike Iraq because U.S. interests matched global security needs. Rejecting the lessons of Vietnam, the president and his top advisers saw no limits to American power as an instrument of global transformation. They also believed that the United States would be welcomed as a liberator in Iraq, and that once victory was secured there, the rest of the Middle East would follow suit because the move toward democracy was the goal of all peoples.

Iraq, then, is not an aberration. Rather, it is part of a pattern of beliefs in U.S. foreign policy grounded in the principle that American ideals are universal and that U.S. power should support and expand those ideals around the globe. What separates Iraq from past American conflicts, however, is the Bush administration's revolutionary goal of democracy promotion through unilateral, preemptive military action. Few presidents have engaged in a war of choice to promote democracy because the linking of power and ideals—democracy, freedom, liberty, capitalism—has not always produced the best results. Larger wars for ideas could be long on rhetoric and short on prudent judgment.[1] Still, the Bush White House argued that it could overcome years of realist compromises with tyranny by following the neoconservative agenda. A more muscular foreign policy would include promoting democracy in the Middle East, by force if necessary. The confidence in the power of the United States to expand American ideals required the Bush administration to reject any lessons that Vietnam had to offer. Instead of viewing the war in Vietnam as an example of the limits of American power, the Bush White House believed Vietnam was a warning that policymakers had to have the right dedication to victory. Therefore, confidence about the mission in Iraq was a fundamental tenet of Bush's foreign policy.

Despite the Bush administration's more incendiary foreign-policy objectives, Congress treated war resolutions on Iraq and Vietnam similarly. In both wars, Congress granted the president unusual authority to wage war in its name. And within months of the start of the wars, the original justification had been discredited. In each case, this discrediting of the justification did not lead to a careful policy review. Instead, as the history of both conflicts shows, U.S. policymakers in the White House rejected carefully calibrated debates about U.S. security interests in favor of idealistic appeals for war. If Vietnam and Iraq can teach us anything about the way the United States goes to war, it is that Congress should insist on a full and frank debate before giving the president broad authority to wage war. Congress should better learn how to discipline power and harness fear. The presidency has grown increasingly imperious over the last several decades, and it is now time for Congress to take its rightful place in the foreign-policy process or risk more misadventures.

The Build-Up to Vietnam: From the Domino Theory to the Doctrine of Credibility

It was, after all, the fear of falling dominos and lofty rhetoric about America's moral obligation to oppose communist aggression that led to the Vietnam War. Despite the nation's enormous military power and strategic dominance, many U.S. policymakers feared that the communists could marshal greater force or be more seductive than a democratic country. Eisenhower's secretary of state, John Foster Dulles, saw the cold war in apocalyptic terms that pitted the forces of good against the forces of evil. He was convinced the United States had to combat atheistic communism with all its military might because the communists knew no moral law and would stop at nothing in their quest for world domination. For Dulles, Christian ideals provided the dynamic difference between success and failure in the set-piece battle against communism. He argued that the only hope of defeating the Soviets and Chinese lay in "reacting with a faith of our own." Dulles was firm in his convictions. "If history teaches us anything," he concluded, "it is that no nation is strong unless its people are imbued with a faith. . . . The impact of the dynamic upon the static . . . will always destroy what it attacks."[2]

The domino theory and a sense of messianic mission drew the United States to war in Vietnam. The conflict was not a quagmire in the 1950s but rather a noble mission in the eyes of the Eisenhower administration to save Southeast Asia from communism. U.S. leaders were so confident about the righteousness of their cause that on several occasions they failed to ask serious questions about the limits of U.S. power or the legitimacy of the domino theory. Support for the Eisenhower position in Vietnam was universal; Democrats and Republicans in both houses of Congress stood behind the domino theory. Senator John F. Kennedy, speaking before the American Friends of Vietnam in 1956, warned that Indochina "represents the cornerstone of the Free World in Southeast Asia, the keystone to the arch, the finger in the dike. Burma, Thailand, India, Japan, the Philippines and obviously Laos and Cambodia are among those whose security would be threatened if the red tide of Communism overflowed into Vietnam."[3]

So confident was the United States in its moral and military position that it rejected any political settlement of the growing crisis in

Vietnam. By 1954, the French government had grown weary of its war against Ho Chi Minh's communists for political control of Vietnam. The French had first come to Indochina in the 1850s, seeking an Asian jewel for their imperial crown. After one hundred years of colonial rule, Paris signed an armistice with the Vietnamese communists at a conference in Geneva that promised a French withdrawal and unifying national elections in Vietnam. The Eisenhower administration rejected the Geneva Accords, however, believing the United States could fare better than the French against the communists because it was not burdened by a colonial past and because providence was on its side.[4] Accordingly, the United States presided over the birth of the Republic of Vietnam, or South Vietnam, as a counter-revolutionary alternative to Ho Chi Minh's communists. Dulles and Eisenhower therefore linked the American mission in Vietnam with American ideals. Anticommunism and the promotion of democracy along liberal lines were both a justification for war and the cornerstone of U.S. ideology.

In 1961 the new Kennedy administration engaged in a formal policy review of its options in Vietnam. Kennedy had been a longtime supporter of the domino theory and was clearly worried about communist advances in newly emerging postcolonial nations in Africa and Asia. The president and his advisers ultimately rejected the domino theory, however, believing there were situational differences in geography that could overcome politics.[5] In other words, Kennedy was less concerned about falling dominos because he no longer believed that they were attached. If one nation fell to communism, it did not automatically mean that neighboring countries would fall. What replaced the domino theory in Kennedy's mind, however, was his new thinking on U.S. credibility, what writer Jonathan Schell appropriately called the "psychological domino theory."[6] Kennedy believed the war in Vietnam was no longer about stopping dominos from falling but rather about showing enemies and allies that the United States lived up to its commitment "to pay any price and bear any burden" . . . to ensure "the survival and success of liberty."[7] Support of South Vietnam, not rolling back communism, became the new goal.

Perhaps Kennedy's two national security secretaries were most forceful in advocating the new policy. Secretary of State Dean Rusk often used protocols of the South East Asia Treaty Organization (SEATO) as sufficient reason for U.S. intervention in Vietnam. According to Rusk, provisions in the 1954 SEATO agreement demanded that the United States come to the defense of any of the signatories.[8] Since South Vietnam had signed this agreement, the United States was obligated by treaty to defend it from communist attacks. Rusk further reasoned that if the United States did not aid South Vietnam, U.S. allies across the globe would come to doubt the U.S. commitment to its treaty obligations. Rusk was particularly worried that U.S. allies in NATO (the North Atlantic Treaty Organization) might wonder if Washington would stand behind that agreement should the Soviets invade another country in Europe. Secretary of Defense Robert S. McNamara argued that if the United States did not intervene in Vietnam, both sides of the Iron Curtain would sense "a major crisis of nerve."[9] In a report to the president, McNamara concluded that "the loss of South Vietnam would . . . undermine the credibility of American commitments elsewhere."[10]

By 1961, according to historian Fred Logevall, the doctrine of credibility had "supplanted the domino theory in American thinking on Vietnam."[11]

LIMITED WAR THEORY

This change in rationale also brought with it a change in strategic thinking. Throughout the Eisenhower years, U.S. foreign policy had been based on the concept of mutually assured destruction (called MAD). The president believed if he built up the American nuclear arsenal so that it could withstand a first strike from the Soviets, Moscow would be deterred from aggressive action. Although the "New Look," as Eisenhower's policy was called, did keep the United States out of major confrontation with the Soviets, it also limited the president's options. Kennedy argued he needed a more flexible policy—one that more accurately reflected the needs of an administration willing to meet the Soviet threat anywhere around the globe. Kennedy envisioned a strategy that would allow the United States to act quickly and decisively against communists in the jungles of Southeast Asia and on the plains in Africa.[12] However, Kennedy did not want these confrontations to lead to a nuclear exchange with the Soviets. Any local war with a country inside the fraternal socialist world system risked a larger war with China or the Soviet Union. Since the Soviet Union possessed nuclear weapons, the balance of terror limited U.S. policymakers in their actions.

At the time, most foreign affairs decisions were seen through the prism of the cold war and the limitations it presented. The primary national security issue of the era was preventing a catastrophic war that might well escalate into a nuclear war with the Soviet Union. The Kennedy administration balanced the need to confront Soviet meddling in newly emerging postcolonial nations with the need to avoid a nuclear exchange with the communist camp through what it called "limited-war theory."

The product of American academics Robert Osgood, Thomas Schelling, and Herman Kahn, limited-war theory gave the president a way to keep wars local and thereby avoid a nuclear showdown.[13] At the heart of this new doctrine was the belief that the president should have the option to respond to Soviet aggression at a low level of violence or through diplomacy. The president could move up the rungs of a ladder of escalation, until such time as the enemy chose to cease and desist its activities rather than face the consequences of further escalation.[14] With enough applied military pressure, according to the theory, the president could communicate with the enemy that it would pay a high price if aggression continued. In the case of Vietnam, the goal was to convince Hanoi that continuing to support the revolution in the south would come at too high a price. Each military escalation, therefore, was a signal to Hanoi to cease and desist. Of course, Hanoi rejected Washington's signals, matching each military escalation with its own.[15]

U.S. fears were not limited to Moscow's cold war power or influence. China was a legitimate threat to American troops in Vietnam. McNamara was convinced during the war that invading North Vietnam with U.S. ground forces carried with it unacceptable risks.[16] He correctly concluded that China would act in its own self-interest and would consider any attack across the seventeenth parallel that divided North Vietnam from South Vietnam an attack against its own borders.[17] General Bruce Palmer, General William Westmoreland's deputy in Vietnam, agreed. He argued in his book *The Twenty-Five Year War* that "one cannot quarrel with the decision not to invade North Vietnam because it was too close to China."[18] U.S. officials now know that North Vietnam asked for and received security commitments from Beijing from 1960 onward.[19] They also know China's Seventh Air Force was moved permanently to the Vietnamese border in case of a ground attack across the seventeenth parallel.[20] Four other air divisions were also moved closer to the border, and Beijing built two airstrips near Lang Son in anticipation of an American invasion.[21] By 1968, over two hundred thousand Chinese troops were serving within North Vietnam's borders.[22]

Kennedy changed not only the rationale for war but also its strategic doctrine. In rejecting the domino theory in favor of the theory of credibility in the struggle against international communism, the president was willing to give up North Vietnam to protect South Vietnam. He was also willing to limit the U.S. military commitment to Vietnam to avoid a larger war that might entice China and the Soviet Union to join the conflict. The second-order issue—protecting South Vietnam from a communist takeover through the application of limited U.S. military pressure—proved more difficult to accomplish than anyone in the Kennedy administration had originally thought. The South Vietnamese government of president Ngo Dinh Diem was corrupt, inefficient, and not very democratic. Diem did little to reach out to those who were in the minority view on some issues.[23] He persecuted Buddhists, believing that they were sympathetic to the communist cause, he rejected land reform programs supported by the United States, and he closed down newspapers that were critical of his rule.[24]

EXPANSION OR WITHDRAWAL?

By the middle of 1963, a frustrated John F. Kennedy was considering another major policy revision. First on Kennedy's list of things to change in Vietnam was President Diem. Despite some support in his administration for staying the course with Diem and his brother, Ngo Dinh Nhu, there was overwhelming backing for regime change in Saigon.[25] Many Kennedy officials believed the U.S. counterinsurgency war was doomed with Diem at the helm.[26] Others argued that the political war so essential to victory was being lost every day because Diem cared little for the village war or for peasants caught in the conflict.[27] What Kennedy envisioned for Diem is still debatable; perhaps he believed the South Vietnamese president would be replaced in a bloodless coup. In the end, however, Diem's own officers executed him and his brother in the back of an armored personnel carrier.

After Diem's assassination, events in Saigon spun out of control. Various political groups wrestled for power in the capital, and the communists made significant advances in the countryside. In fact, the Communist Party hoped to take advantage of the chaos in Saigon. At its December 1963 plenum, party leaders agreed to "escalate the level of armed struggle in the South."[28] According to party leaders, "Armed struggle would be the direct and deciding factor in the annihilation of the armed forces of the enemy."[29] Le Duan, the party's secretary general and a longtime advocate of a more forceful military policy in South Vietnam, applauded the decision.

As Hanoi turned up the heat, the Kennedy administration considered its options. One option was to withdraw. Convinced South Vietnam would eventually "throw our asses out," and needing to score some political points without a huge military cost, Kennedy had considered a limited withdrawal as early as 1962.[30] By April 1963, some administration officials suggested that withdrawing a thousand U.S. advisers "out of the blue" would reassure the American public the war was going well and would undercut the communists' "best propaganda line," that the United States was running the war for South Vietnam.[31] Kennedy had McNamara draw up the plans for the limited withdrawal to begin in December 1963. Many believed the president was starting to phase out U.S. operations in Vietnam, and that after the 1964 presidential election he would withdraw all U.S. advisers. McNamara went on record stating he was convinced Kennedy would have withdrawn U.S. forces had he been reelected.[32] No one will ever know. Kennedy was assassinated on November 22, 1963.

Of course, Kennedy had another option, which was to intervene more forcefully. With just over sixteen thousand U.S. advisers in Vietnam, it was clear that more could be done to prop up the Saigon government and to aid the South Vietnamese armed forces. From the earliest days of the administration, some of Kennedy's key advisers had advocated a more militant line.[33] By the summer of 1963 many were calling for the president to introduce U.S. ground troops to take over the war from the South Vietnamese forces and to save Saigon from total defeat.[34] Others suggested that a strong air campaign over North Vietnam would take some pressure off South Vietnam.[35] It now seems clear Kennedy refused to ask the hard questions about American intervention in Vietnam, content instead to continue to steer a middle course that promised neither withdrawal nor greater involvement.

When Lyndon B. Johnson entered the Oval Office, he, too, could have expanded the war or withdrawn. In typical Johnson fashion, he chose neither course. Always wanting to keep his options open, Johnson usually took the path that limited his policy choices. The president and his national security advisers decided to continue Kennedy's commitment to the defense of South Vietnam and to keep America's role in the war limited. On March 17, 1964, Johnson outlined his decision in what is now known as National Security Memorandum No. 288.[36] Expanding on Kennedy's redefinition of the war's aims, Johnson argued that nothing short of U.S. credibility was at stake in Vietnam. The administration would continue to support South Vietnam in its hour of need, the president concluded, because the United States was the only power that could do so. In the face of danger, the United States never backed down. Rusk perhaps put it best when he argued that the "integrity of the U.S. commitment is the principal pillar of peace throughout the world. If that commitment becomes unreliable, the communist world would draw conclusions that would lead to our ruin and almost certainly to a catastrophic war."[37] America's war aims in Vietnam during the Johnson years were still focused on containment and credibility.

Thus, U.S. goals in the Kennedy and Johnson years were counterrevolutionary. First, the United States wanted to stop the spread of communism in Southeast Asia, and then, after rejecting the domino theory, U.S. policymakers wanted to stop the communists from taking over South Vietnam. As the war dragged on, the chief goal became convincing enemies and allies that the United States honored its treaty commitments. Credibility was as important as the specific military mission. Containment, preservation, and credibility were the hallmarks of America's war aims in Vietnam. Only in building up South Vietnam as a viable alternative to Ho Chi Minh's communists did the United States move from the defensive to the offensive.

THE BUILD-UP TO IRAQ: FROM WEAPONS OF
MASS DESTRUCTION TO THE WAR ON TERROR

The Iraq War, in sharp contrast, is revolutionary. Its war aims include effecting regime change, spreading democracy in the region, and destroying an international terrorist network. The rationale for such a radical agenda began in early 2003, when Colin Powell, then Bush's secretary of state, appeared before the United Nations (UN). Powell argued that Saddam Hussein was taunting the United Nations and its various resolutions urging him to comply with weapons inspections.[38] If the UN was to have any relevance, Powell argued, it needed to pass a Security Council resolution authorizing military strikes against Iraq, as it had done in the first Gulf War (1990–1991). Short of that, Powell warned, the United States was prepared to go it alone because its strength was beyond challenge and there was a monster out there to destroy. According to Powell, Hussein was developing weapons of mass destruction to "project power, to threaten, and to deliver chemical, biological and, if we let him, nuclear warheads."[39] He also indicated that a second-order issue for the Bush administration was a "sinister nexus between Iraq and the Al Qaeda terrorist network, a nexus that combines classic terrorist organizations and modern methods of murder."[40]

For nearly a year before Powell's UN speech, President George W. Bush had been delivering the same message. In 2002 he argued the United States had a responsibility to change the course of events in Iraq because the threat from that country "stands alone" and because it "gathers the most serious dangers of our age in one place."[41] When no weapons of mass destruction were found in Iraq following the March 2003 invasion, the Bush administration shifted its war rationale completely to the war on terror and promoting democracy in the region. Bush and his national security team then argued that the insurgency in Iraq was led by Osama bin Laden and his Jordanian subcontractor Abu Musab al-Zarkawi. They suggested that the only thing that kept the insurgency alive was the cross-border invasion of Iraq by these radical elements. Despite the growing evidence that much of the insurgency is directed by Sunni rebels and former allies of Saddam Hussein inside Iraq, and that much of the violence is the result of Shiite counterattacks in certain strongholds, like Moqtada al-Sadr's Mahdi Army in Najaf, the Bush administration continues to make the connection between events in Iraq and the al-Qaeda network.

THE BUSH DOCTRINE AND THE NEOCONS

The war on terror was spelled out specifically in what is now known as the Bush Doctrine. Originally outlined in the president's graduation address in June 2002 at West Point, the Bush Doctrine was formally delineated in the president's report on *The National Security Strategy of the United States of America* (NSS), released September 17, 2002.[42] In this document, the Bush administration outlined its ambitious and comprehensive grand strategy: "We will defend the peace by fighting terrorists and tyrants. We will preserve the peace by building good relations among the great powers. We will extend the peace by encouraging free and open societies on every continent."[43] The Bush Doctrine also pledges that the United States "will identify and eliminate terrorists wherever they are, together with the regimes that sustain them."[44] Following the direction of nineteenth-century U.S. leaders, Bush pledged to launch preemptive strikes against the enemy before its forces could attack the United States. Unlike most other presidents, with the exception of Franklin D. Roosevelt and James Madison, however, Bush had tangible evidence of the destructive capacity of America's enemies if left unchallenged.

Given the president's strategy to attack America's enemies first, what propelled the Bush administration to invade Iraq? In many ways, Iraq was the most secular country in the region, and not one terrorist from the September 11 attacks was an Iraqi. Still, Bush found compelling reasons for Iraq to put the Bush Doctrine in action. An attack against Iraq could topple a tyrant, showing the rest of the world that the United States would not sit by and watch the evil wield power. By defeating Saddam sufficiently, the Bush administration hoped to shatter the dreams of others who wished the United States harm. An attack against Iraq could also finish the job started in the first Gulf War, when the United States launched a counterattack against Saddam to force him to exit Kuwait. Some have suggested President Bush was highly influenced by Elliot Cohen's book *Supreme Command,* which was critical of George H.W. Bush (Bush I) for not taking Baghdad at the end of the first Gulf War.[45] Attacking Iraq also promised to root out the terrorists whom Bush believed Saddam had been supporting all along.

At the core of the Bush administration's rationale for invading Iraq lay also the belief that the United States needed to attack the conditions that had led to the rise of terrorists. Bush and his closest advisers believed the nation needed to promote democracy in the Middle East because it was the lack of representative institutions within Arab societies that drove terrorists to drastic measures. The attacks of September 11 were led by middle-class, relatively well-educated men who came from countries with no democratic traditions, Bush reasoned, and therefore had no outlet for their political grievances. Starting with Iraq, the United States would plant the seeds of democracy and watch them grow. For Bush, democracy itself was a transformative power, and its expansion in the Middle East promised to make the United States more secure. With new democratic institutions, the Arab middle class would take ownership of the political process alongside the traditional royal families and authoritarian regimes. Shared power through a more democratic state, Bush believed, could transform the Middle East from an unpredictable and potentially dangerous region into a stable and peaceful one. The Bush administration firmly believed that history was on the side of democratic states and that Washington had an obligation to use its considerable power to bring about democratic change.

The chief architect of this policy was Paul Wolfowitz, at that time Bush's deputy secretary of defense. Wolfowitz had had a long and distinguished career in government before joining the Bush administration, first working for U.S. Senator Henry "Scoop" Jackson (D-Washington) as an aide and later with Fred Ikle, the director of the U.S. Arms Control and Disarmament Agency. In the latter post, Wolfowitz had become one the most important members of "Team B," a committee designed to assess the Soviet threat. Team B challenged many of Henry Kissinger's beliefs about Soviet intentions and capabilities, suggesting that the U.S. policy of détente had distracted American policymakers from Moscow's "darker side."[46] During the Carter years, Wolfowitz moved to the Pentagon, where he would return after a Clinton-era sabbatical as the dean of the Paul Nitze School at Johns Hopkins University and ambassador to Indonesia. He became Bush's deputy secretary for defense in 2001.

Many of Wolfowitz's ideas came from neoconservative thinking that had developed over the course of the twentieth century. This neoconservatism had taken root among a small group of intellectuals, based mainly in New York in the late 1930s. That group included Irving Kristol, Daniel Bell, Irving Howe, and Nathan Glazer. Early in their adult lives, these young men were attracted to the writings of Leon Trotsky. They believed in social progress and the universality of rights but feared that communism under Stalin had grown excessive. Over time, they grew more critical of communism in general. By the late 1940s, their ideas were cemented around the belief that all totalitarian regimes would crumble if pushed hard enough. In 1989 and 1991, the neoconservatives celebrated the end of the cold war and the collapse of the Soviet Union. In their book *Present Dangers,* two leading neoconservatives, William Kristol and Robert Kagan, argued that the victory over the Soviets and the Eastern European bloc could be repeated if the United States was willing to add muscle to its foreign policy. They wrote, "To many the idea of America using its power to promote changes of regimes in nations ruled by dictators rings of utopianism. But in fact, it is eminently realistic. There is something perverse in declaring the impossibility of promoting democratic change abroad in light of the record of the past three decades."[47] Following Kristol and Kagan's logic, Wolfowitz believed regime change was possible in Iraq. He also supported the neoconservative idea that there was a universal hunger for liberty in all people and that they would rise up to support democratic challenges to dictatorial regimes.

After the September 11 attacks, therefore, Wolfowitz called on the Bush administration to launch preemptive strikes against Iraq as well as to intervene directly in Afghanistan.[48] He also suggested that the global war against terror be seen as a global war for freedom.[49] Liberating Iraq would be the first step in democratizing the Middle East. Since the Arab Street respects force, Wolfowitz reasoned, the United States should link its power with its mission. He knowingly committed the United States to a broader and heavily militarized strategy of liberating the entire Islamic world. Unlike in Southeast Asia at the time of the Vietnam War, the dominos would fall in the Middle East, but in the opposite direction. After Iraq, the rest of the Middle East would be up for grabs. These radical ideas remained the cornerstone of the Bush administration's policy in Iraq well into 2008, even though Wolfowitz had left the Pentagon to become president of the World Bank in 2005. Despite soaring rhetoric about exporting democracy, the reality facing the Bush administration in its last year in power is a little more sobering. Instead of a regional map showing the flowering of democracy, President Bush looks at local maps of Baghdad and Anbar province, hoping to secure a few more blocks. The grand strategic thinking about spreading democracy abroad has given way to a more harsh reality.

EXPORTING AMERICAN IDEALS

In many ways, the Bush administration has pushed to the limit its idea that exporting democracy makes America more secure. Unlike the counterrevolutionary strategy pursued in Vietnam, the revolutionary promotion of democracy in the Middle East began with a war of choice. In Vietnam, the argument can certainly be made that there were legitimate threats to American interests in the region and that the Chinese were indeed supporting the Vietnamese revolution with personnel, material, and advice. From the earliest days of the Vietnam War, few policymakers in Washington believed that the conflict was about promoting democracy in South Vietnam. In a now famous memorandum written by John McNaughton, McNamara's deputy on the war, the White House supported the idea that only "ten percent" of the reason for the United States to intervene in Vietnam was to "permit the people of SVN [South Vietnam] to enjoy a better, freer way of life."[50] In Iraq, however, the Bush administration's policies have been more expansive, even radical, in their strategic thinking. The White House has consistently argued that the United States can indeed mold the world in its image.

This idea has deep historical roots. Jefferson called the expansion of U.S. ideals essential for the survival of the "empire of liberty."[51] He saw no contradiction between the creation of an empire and liberty. He believed that an expanding liberal empire was actually the best safeguard of liberty. Woodrow Wilson called such an expansion making the world safe for democracy.[52] Inside Wilson's liberalism was the belief that autocrats, like the German kaiser, had wrested freedom from their people. Once these autocrats were destroyed, the people could create liberal, democratic governments. Wilson also believed that a world unencumbered by imperialism and revolution would favor American security and prosperity. These principles lay behind Wilson's willingness to take the nation to war in Europe, even though most Americans saw that war as a conflict between competing imperial empires that need not affect the United States. Wilson saw it differently. He believed that the peace following such a war held out the potential to create a new world order. From the ashes of old Europe, the United States could rebuild the international community on American principles.[53] The right to self-determination would force the collapse of empires, and free markets and humanized capitalism would ensure American-style democracy. For Wilson, then, free people would naturally want American democracy. It was his obligation to give it to them.

Lyndon Johnson also believed in exporting American ideals. Where George W. Bush has envisioned new democratic institutions to harness anger and frustration abroad, Johnson saw access to resources and economic opportunity as the keys to security and stability. As a young U.S. senator, Johnson had supported Franklin Roosevelt's New Deal programs, believing the government had a responsibility to end poverty and want. He had an emotional attachment to the New Deal and its liberal philosophy because as a young man in Texas, he had seen what Roosevelt's program could do. He was particularly attracted to the programs of the Tennessee Valley Authority (TVA), which dammed rivers and lakes to provide electricity to the Deep South. "Where I live," Johnson was fond of saying, "I have seen the night illuminated, and the kitchen warmed, and the home heated, where once the cheerless night and the ceaseless cold held sway. And all this happened because electricity came to our area along the humming wires of the REA (Rural Electrification Administration), a part of the TVA."[54]

In Vietnam, Johnson believed that it was his responsibility to do more than simply stop the spread of communism. He also believed that it was essential to show that what had worked for America during the 1930s depression would work in Vietnam. Johnson argued that the United States had the "power" and the "opportunity" to "improve the life of man in that conflict-torn corner of the world."[55]

In a speech at Johns Hopkins University in April 1965, one month after the first U.S. ground troops landed in Vietnam, Johnson promised that the war could end tomorrow if only Hanoi would embrace Johnson's liberal philosophy in an effort to help its own people the way the New Deal had helped Americans. The president offered that the United States was ready to help the Vietnamese overcome "the bondage of material misery" if they would only put the war aside.[56] The United States could be a force for great economic change in Vietnam, if only Ho would let it.

The cornerstone of Johnson's New Deal for Vietnam was a bold economic development plan along the lines of the Tennessee Valley Authority. Johnson pledged $1 billion to create a Mekong River Development Project that would harness that mighty river's power to bring cheap electricity and economic development to Vietnam.[57] "Old Ho can't turn me down," Johnson told aide Bill Moyers after Johnson's proposal had been carried on nationwide television.[58] For Johnson, the promise of government had always been its transformative powers. In the area of foreign relations, the inexperienced Johnson saw everything through the eyes of that Texas boy who had marveled at the light. He wanted to "leave the footprints of America in Vietnam," along with the lasting belief that "when Americans come, this is what they leave—schools, not long cigars. We're going to turn the Mekong into a Tennessee Valley."[59]

For Johnson, exporting the best of what America had to offer was the answer to the most pressing problems in Vietnam. The same premise holds for Bush's efforts in Iraq, though the Bush administration has rejected Johnson's focus on state modernization and economic development in favor of privatization and free-market solutions to nation building. But as both men were to discover, neither tactic delivered a stable ally. Furthermore, five years into the nation-building experiment in Iraq, there seems to be sufficient evidence that terrorism did not originate from the absence of democracy alone. It may be that the very values that Bush is trying to export remain a primary target for most terrorists, as Samuel Huntington has argued.[60] Or it may be that ethnic, religious, and tribal differences *within* Iraq are the source of violence. The conflict may not be a clash of civilizations, but rather, as John Lewis Gaddis and others have noted, it may be a clash within a civilization that fuels the fire of hatred.[61] Is the Islamic world struggling with itself to determine what kind of future it wants? Is there such a thing as the Islamic world? The Bush administration's insistence on democracy promotion and privatization in Iraq has found few takers. The region is in more chaos now than it has been in recent memory, and instead of the flowering of democracy, it appears, more autocratic forms of government are what is in store for the Middle East.

For Lyndon Johnson, giving the Mekong Delta a New Deal facelift was equally problematic. The communists ignored his pleas to consider economic growth and development instead of war. Johnson, hopelessly out of touch with the realities of rural Vietnam, believed that everyone worldwide would embrace his New Deal. When Hanoi rejected his overtures, Johnson was crushed. He reportedly told aide Jack Valenti that Ho was out of his mind for choosing bombs over economic development. "My God, I've offered Ho Chi Minh $100 million to build a Mekong Valley. If that'd been George Meany he'd have snapped at it!"[62] The communists turned their back on the one thing that Johnson knew worked: government-funded economic development programs. Johnson's hope of channeling the radical Vietnamese revolution along liberal New Deal lines was further evidence of the huge cultural gap between the United States and Vietnam. National liberation and socialist development, not economic development along capitalist lines, were the primary goals of the Vietnamese revolution. Eventually, Johnson's own allies in Saigon would spurn similar projects. The president left the White House in 1969, still wondering why the Vietnamese had not grasped the significance of his offer. For Johnson, Hanoi's refusal to cooperate with him on a New Deal for Vietnam left him few options.

Whether seeking to expand the security of American institutions by spreading them abroad or using such ideals as a cover for aggression, Bush and Johnson did not take the United States to a war footing alone. Congress agreed in both cases to give the president unbridled authority to wage war without declaring it. Members of Congress in both houses overwhelmingly supported the two presidents' war aims and agreed that the missions in Vietnam and Iraq were worth American blood and treasure.

Preparing the Country for War in Vietnam

In August 1964, Congress gave Lyndon Johnson broad presidential authority to use any means necessary to put down communist aggression in Vietnam.[63] The Congress was responding to claims by the Johnson administration that North Vietnamese torpedo boats had fired on U.S. destroyers patrolling international waters. On the afternoon of August 2, 1964, the destroyer USS *Maddox* was on a secret mission in the Tonkin Gulf, near North Vietnam's coastline. The

Maddox was part of a larger flotilla that had launched attacks against the nearby island of Hon Me. South Vietnamese gunboats had launched the attacks, in part to see how North Vietnam would respond. They found out soon enough as North Vietnamese torpedo boats attacked the *Maddox*. After a brief exchange of fire, the torpedo boats were driven away.[64]

News of the attacks enraged Johnson, but he ordered no new retaliation. Instead, Johnson agreed with the Joint Chiefs of Staff, who argued that the *Maddox* should resume its operations in the Gulf of Tonkin. The U.S. Navy also ordered another destroyer, the *Turner Joy*, to the gulf to support the *Maddox*. The administration kept the destroyers near the North Vietnamese coast, hoping to draw the communists into another exchange. According to historian George C. Herring, some military officials were so eager to go to war against North Vietnam that they "were choosing targets for retaliatory raids before reports of a second attack began to come in."[65] They soon got their wish. On the night of August 4, while operating in heavy seas sixty miles off the North Vietnamese coast, the *Maddox* and the *Turner Joy* reported new attacks. Sonar and radar reports confirmed that North Vietnamese gunboats were in the area and had fired torpedoes.[66]

Almost immediately, key members of the Johnson administration called for swift and decisive action against North Vietnam. McNamara argued that the United States could not "sit still as a nation and let them attack us on the high seas and get away with it."[67] Dean Rusk believed that if the United States did not respond with considerable force, the world would think it was a "paper tiger."[68] The Joint Chiefs insisted Johnson respond immediately with retaliatory air strikes aimed at the heart of North Vietnam's war production facilities and naval shipyards.[69]

Only the Central Intelligence Agency (CIA) urged caution, suggesting that Hanoi might have been acting out of pride and defensively to the raids on Hon Me island.[70] Johnson dismissed the CIA's argument, opting instead for a "firm, swift retaliatory strike" against North Vietnamese torpedo bases and oil storage dumps.[71]

Ignoring new evidence brought forward on the afternoon of August 4, which suggested that a second attack had not occurred, Johnson accepted the recommendation of the commander in chief of the Pacific fleet, Admiral U.S. Grant Sharp, to launch the attack.[72] By that evening, U.S. air strikes had destroyed twenty-five North Vietnamese patrol boats and an oil storage facility in Ho Chi Minh's hometown of Vinh. Johnson went on nationwide television to tell the American people of the North Vietnamese attacks and the U.S. response. The president recounted the events of the past two days, stating that hostile North Vietnamese actions against the *Maddox* and the *Turner Joy* had forced him "to order the military forces of the United States to take action in reply."[73] Johnson concluded his remarks by assuring his listeners that the United States was right to respond with strength. "Firmness in the right is indispensable today for peace. That firmness will always be measured. Its mission is peace."[74]

Thirty years later in Hanoi, I sat next to Robert S. McNamara and General Vo Nguyen Giap when the Vietnamese military leader told Johnson's secretary of defense that no second attack had occurred. McNamara was convinced by Giap's explanation and included that exchange in his lessons on how to avoid conflict in the future.[75] It now seems clear that no second attack did occur, even though it is doubtful that McNamara purposefully deceived the president. More likely, an administration itching for war took limited intelligence information as a clear sign of aggression because such a sign was what it had wanted all along. For months, the Johnson administration had been exploring its options in Vietnam, hoping to find some way to save South Vietnam from complete collapse. The coup against Diem in November 1963 had created chaos in Saigon, and the communists had increased their military pressure to deal a deathblow to South Vietnam. By the summer of 1964 several key members of the Johnson administration had favored a direct attack against North Vietnam to save South Vietnam.[76] The Gulf of Tonkin attacks, therefore, came at a favorable time and provided the pretext for a larger war.

Following his television address, Johnson asked Congress for a resolution that gave him full power to respond to the communists in Vietnam. The resolution authorized the president to take "all necessary measures to repel any armed attacks against the forces of the United States and to prevent further aggression."[77] Short of a declaration of war, the Tonkin Gulf Resolution united the nation behind more aggressive action in Vietnam. With limited debate, in fewer than ten hours, the U.S. Senate overwhelmingly approved the measure. Only Senators Wayne Morse (D-Oregon) and Ernest Gruening (D-Alaska) voted against the resolution. In the House, the debate lasted an unbelievably brief forty minutes and the measure passed unanimously.[78]

Many members of Congress beat the war drum along with Johnson. Ross Adair, a Republican in the House from Indiana, claimed that "the American flag had been fired upon." He declared that the United States "cannot tolerate such things."[79] Senator J. William Fulbright (D-Arkansas), chair of the Senate Foreign Relations Committee, agreed. The skillful senator steered Johnson's resolution through the Senate, stressing the Senate's patriotic duty and the president's caution. He urged his colleagues to think of the resolution as a moderate measure "calculated to prevent the spread of war."[80] He argued that the president would consult Congress before enlarging the war, and he assured his fellow senators that "no one wanted another land war in Asia."[81] Fulbright also reminded his colleagues it was an election year, and the Democratic-controlled Congress did not want to spar with their party's president shortly before national elections.

Johnson was pleased with the broad authority given to him by Congress. "Like grandma's nightshirt," he later joked, "it covered everything."[82] Overnight the president's approval ratings went up 30 percent.[83] Congress and the American public had spoken. They supported the president, his war aims, and his belief that the United States would be more secure with limited but strategic attacks on the communists. Drawing on earlier U.S. formulations of preemption and expansion, the Johnson administration took the nation to war in Vietnam to protect perceived U.S. interests, ideals, and borders. The common impulse in U.S. foreign relations to strike out against an adversary before it can strike at you overwhelmed any potential debate inside the administration, in the Congress, or among the American people. As Johnson went to war, he had expanded presidential power with the full support of the vast majority of the American public. The same was true of George W. Bush.

THE RUSH TO WAR IN IRAQ

Shortly before Colin Powell's testimony at the United Nations in February 2003, the Bush administration moved quickly to gain support for its war aims, in Congress and from the American people. On

September 4, 2002, Bush sent a letter to key members of Congress suggesting that he would soon seek that body's support for action in Iraq. The president said he needed to consult with Congress to figure out "how to disarm an outlaw regime."[84] Bush maintained that following the first Gulf War, Saddam Hussein had remained a "threat to peace."[85] Particularly upsetting to Bush was Hussein's refusal to cooperate with UN weapons inspectors. According to the president, Baghdad had defied at least sixteen UN resolutions. Bush suggested that Iraq was hiding something, and that it was up to the United States to find out what that was. He feared that Hussein was seeking weapons of mass destruction to use against the United States and Israel as he had against his own people. The president pledged his administration's cooperation with Congress as it held hearings to come to terms with Iraq.

During those hearings, Bush officials focused on two key items: weapons of mass destruction and Iraq's support of terrorists. The president's key advisers testified that Saddam Hussein had used lethal gas against his own people and that he was obviously developing new weapons to use against the United States and Israel. Furthermore, the administration claimed, Iraq was now harboring an international terrorist network that included many members of Osama Bin Laden's al-Qaeda team. Although the evidence to support such claims was shaky at best, administration officials testified that the president believed Iraq was now a direct threat to the security of the United States. Some members of Congress balked at the administration's claims, but most were convinced by the president's message.

Eventually, Congress gave the president the war resolution he had been seeking. On October 9, 2002, both houses of Congress passed

H.J. 114, authorizing the president to "use the Armed Forces of the United States as he determines to be necessary and appropriate in order to defend the national security of the United States against the continued threat posed by Iraq" and to "enforce all relevant United Nations Security Council resolutions regarding Iraq."[86] Careful not to give Bush a blank check in Iraq, Congress did place limits on the president's actions. The resolution required the president to consult Congress within forty-eight hours of taking direct military action in Iraq and to report on the war's progress to the appropriate congressional committees every sixty days.[87] Like Johnson before him, President Bush received bipartisan support for the war resolution. Key Democrats voted in favor of the resolution, including Senator John Kerry, Bush's 2004 presidential election opponent, and Senators Hillary Clinton and John McCain, both presidential hopefuls in 2008. Most members of Congress believed, as Senator McCain did, that the president's team had made "a convincing case" against Iraq. Tom DeLay, Republican Majority Leader of the House, concluded during the congressional debate that "military action is inevitable."[88]

A small minority in Congress opposed the resolution. Senator Robert Byrd (D-West Virginia) argued that it gave the president "unchecked authority." Senator Edward Kennedy (D-Massachusetts) concluded that only Congress could declare war. He worried that Congress was giving the president too much power for war in advance. Few of the protests concerned the invasion itself. Most, like Byrd and Kennedy, looked to the constitutional issue. Richard Gephardt, one of the authors of the resolution, had once been a Democratic presidential hopeful.[89] By fall 2002 he was helping a Republican president gain broad war powers from Congress. Senate

Minority Leader Tom Daschle, a Vietnam veteran and usually an outspoken critic of the Bush administration, also supported the measure.[90] In the end, the Senate passed the House version of the resolution without changing a single word.

The congressional resolution safely tucked in his pocket, President Bush then went to the American people to gain their support. In his most important public speech on Iraq, his State of the Union address on January 28, 2003, President Bush gave his first hard evidence that Iraq was trying to obtain weapons of mass destruction. In what is now referred to as the "infamous 16 words," Bush declared, "The British government has learned that Saddam Hussein recently sought significant quantities of uranium from Africa."[91] For the first time, Bush made the connection between Iraq and weapons of mass destruction. Furthermore, Bush also made a convincing argument that Iraq had harbored terrorists since the ending of the first Gulf War. With successful strikes in Afghanistan against key terrorist networks in 2002, many of America's sworn enemies were now operating inside Iraq, according to Bush, with Saddam Hussein's support and approval. In public opinion polls across the United States following the speech, an overwhelming majority of the American people favored a direct strike against Iraq before it could attack the United States.[92]

With Congress and the American public on board, Bush moved to secure support from the United Nations and the international community. Powell's speech before the UN in February 2003 was designed to produce a Security Council resolution against Iraq much like the one used to justify coalition attacks against Baghdad in the first Gulf War. When the Security Council refused to adopt such a resolution, Secretary of Defense Donald Rumsfeld suggested that the United States did not need "old Europe" to defend its interests, a thinly veiled attack on the French, who had opposed the UN resolution forcefully.[93] Of the major U.S. allies, only Britain's Tony Blair supported the United States and its desire for regime change in Iraq.

In short, by the time of the March 2003 invasion of Iraq, the Bush administration had a congressional resolution authorizing the attack, a major ally by its side, and the support of the American people.

Just as in Vietnam, however, the rush to war had precluded significant debate. With the resolution vote held just one month before the 2002 midterm elections, few members of Congress wanted to openly challenge the president and the majority party. Furthermore, just as in Vietnam, the major reason for action turned out to be quickly discredited. There had been no provocative second attack in the Tonkin Gulf, and there were no weapons of mass destruction in Iraq. Even the one piece of hard evidence that the Bush administration offered to link Baghdad with nuclear weapons vanished when it was discovered that the British report making the connection between Iraq and a source of uranium in Africa had been fabricated. Thus, both wars were built on the misreading of important security information. More important, however, in Vietnam and Iraq, both presidents had the support of Congress as they marched to war.

THE EMPHASIS ON RHETORIC OVER DEBATE

Vietnam and Iraq were not the first attempts by the president to use a congressional fig leaf for waging war. In 1798, John Adams used executive power to maneuver the United States toward an undeclared

war with France. James Madison used presidential authority to sub-
vert and then seize West Florida in what some historians have called
the earliest analogue to the Gulf of Tonkin Resolution.[94] James K.
Polk asked Congress for a declaration of war against Mexico after he
had forced a military confrontation. Yet Vietnam and Iraq clearly
illustrate the changing nature of the relationship between Congress
and the president in the context of war. Even after experiencing Vietnam and the growing power of the presidency, Congress neverthe-
less repealed the War Powers Act and restored unusual authority to
the president.

The main problem in Iraq, as in Vietnam, was that it was relatively easy for the president to speak to ideals and not interests when
laying out his war plan before Congress and the American people.
Heightened threat perceptions and the uniquely American impulse
to strike out against potential adversaries led the United States to
war in Iraq and Vietnam. In both wars, fear and the appeal to ideals
all but completely quashed debate. It is remarkable that most members of Congress waited until the 2006 midterm elections to voice
any serious opposition to the president's policies in Iraq. Congress
finally held hearings in January 2007 to consider the Iraq Study
Group Report, but even these deliberations were more publicity
events than serious inquiry. Not one major policy revision came out
of these investigations. And in the last year of the Bush presidency,
the Democratically controlled Congress now seems intent on waiting
for a new president before it passes any binding resolutions on Iraq.

In both Iraq and Vietnam, the United States went to war under
the cloud of insecurity. Fearful that communism was on the march
or that terrorists might strike at any moment, U.S. policymakers

used exalted rhetoric to convince ordinary Americans that national security issues were at stake. Preemption and expansion promised to eliminate threats and make the world a more stable place. In this sense, Iraq and Vietnam are clearly in the U.S. foreign policy tradition. What separates Iraq from Vietnam and other wars, however, is the revolutionary nature of the Bush administration's policies. Without a clear connection between Iraq and the terrorists who attacked the United States on September 11, it remains hard to justify a war of choice that has not spread democracy but left a region in chaos and perhaps created a failed state.

Given the trajectory of events in Vietnam and Iraq, it is clear that the White House and Congress should have debated the war resolutions more forcefully. In both cases, a debate daily for a full month or more would not have jeopardized American security or national interests. Debate should have been measured in terms of days and weeks, not hours. Indeed, the Senate debated making Martin Luther King's birthday a national holiday two weeks longer than it debated either the Gulf of Tonkin Resolution or the resolution authorizing the Bush administration to invade Iraq.[95] When national security is not at stake, it is always better to have a full and frank debate than to rush to war. Extensive debate grounded in caution and insight could have uncovered important questions about the nature of the wars and the efficacy of committing the nation to war overseas. Certainly the men and women in uniform deserve the nation's best-considered judgment.

Furthermore, the panic-stricken Congress gave the president unusual authority to wage war in Vietnam and Iraq. Without a declaration of war, has Congress clearly spoken? It is much harder to get out of war than to get into it, and these two congressional resolutions paved the way for future problems. In both cases, some members of Congress have argued, the White House deceived them. In both cases, some members of Congress are worried they indeed gave the president too much authority to wage war. And in both cases, it became increasingly difficult for Congress to register its objections to administration policy. The preferred time to debate the rationale for war is before troops are in the field. In both Iraq and Vietnam, Congress should have insisted on a more substantive debate before granting the president a war resolution. In Vietnam, Congress eventually rescinded the president's authority to wage war in its name. Ironically, the more aggressive foreign policies of the Bush administration have had no such review. Instead, Congress seems intent on waiting for a change in government before it will act. This delay will handcuff American foreign policy in the future.

CHAPTER TWO

THE MILITARY HALF

T HERE ARE many military lessons to learn from Vietnam, but the Bush administration has made the deadly mistake of approaching problems in Iraq as if the United States is facing them for the first time. The lack of interest in history in the Bush White House has been mind-boggling and helps explain why this administration has made so many strategic and operational errors. The primary lesson of Vietnam, and one completely ignored by President Bush and his advisers, is that there is often no political corollary to America's overwhelming military power. In Vietnam, the armed forces of the United States fought with courage and valor. They never lost a major military engagement and they inflicted severe pain on their adversaries. Yet U.S. objectives in Vietnam proved illusive. The United States was never able to translate that massive military might into sustainable political results. Without a successful political war, there was little that could be done militarily in Vietnam to change the course of the war within acceptable risks and costs.

Another related lesson of the Vietnam War is that counter-insurgency programs based on pacification—the elimination of military and political elements through coercion, enticements, and assassination—may be effective in eliminating insurgents, but these tactics alone cannot win a war. Many in the Bush White House believed that pacification had worked in Vietnam and therefore should be applied to Iraq. This is a serious misreading of a compli-cated issue. Pacification did eradicate many political and military cadres inside the National Liberation Front (NLF) infrastructure, but it did little to stop the advance of the People's Army of Vietnam (PAVN) inside South Vietnam, and by 1970, PAVN was the major military player in Vietnam. Military and political success in a coun-terinsurgency program cannot be measured by the number of dead insurgents. Without a substantial political program, increasing the level of violence to kill insurgents is often counterproductive and plays into the psychological war plans of the enemy. In an asymmet-rical war of attrition, insurgents will always trade resources for time. Time is the enemy of the more powerful and distant adversary.

And finally, it is absolutely essential to understand the character and nature of the insurgency before you can have any political or military success against it. Early in the Vietnam War, U.S. military planners made the tragic mistake of thinking that Vietnam was just like Korea. They assumed that guerrilla warfare in South Vietnam was just a precursor to a larger, more conventional invasion from North Vietnam. U.S. military planning grew from this set of assump-tions and American advisers trained the South Vietnamese army for this kind of war. This misreading of the southern nature of the in-surgency cost the United States and its allies in Saigon valuable time and gave the communists the strategic upper hand. After these initial mistakes, it was quite difficult for the United States to recover. Because Washington had misread the nature of the southern insurgency so badly in the early years of the war, critics claimed that successive administrations were lying about the ties between the NLF and Hanoi, contributing significantly to the communists' diplomatic strategy. The key lesson here: Know your enemy.

MILITARY OPERATIONS IN VIETNAM

U.S. military operations changed dramatically in Vietnam between 1955 and the war's end in 1975. What began as a slow trickle of American advisers turned into a full-scale conflict with U.S. troop levels in Vietnam peaking in April 1969 at 543,000.[1] American forces included nine U.S. Army and Marine Corps divisions plus several subdivisional combat units. Each year, over 100,000 U.S. troops served in the region as support staff for those in-country personnel. In fact, more Americans served in Vietnam than in any other foreign war in U.S. history, with the exception of World War II. Another 100,000 troops fought in Vietnam each year from U.S. allies, especially South Korea, Thailand, Australia, New Zealand, and the Philippines.[2] Most important, the Republic of Vietnam Armed Forces (RVNAF), America's South Vietnamese allies, fielded over 1 million soldiers at its peak.[3] The high-water mark for allied forces in the field was nearly 1.6 million troops.

Combined communist forces of the PAVN and the People's Liberation Armed Forces (PLAF)—known in the West as the Viet Cong—also numbered well over 1 million soldiers under arms.[4] If the

PLAF's irregular guerrillas and political cadres who carried out strategic violence are added to the total, communist troop levels overall approached those of the United States and its allies. In addition, the 200,000 Chinese combat engineers who served in North Vietnam released PAVN main-force infantry units to the southern battlefield.[5] Soviet advisers were also plentiful in the early years of the war, but their numbers declined substantially after the introduction of U.S. ground troops in March 1965. Hanoi had no problem drawing on its reserves, and it likely could have mobilized nearly 1.5 million soldiers for the final push against Saigon had that been necessary. A compulsory draft law passed in 1958 assured PAVN generals of adequate personnel to meet their force-level requirements for as long as the Americans remained in Vietnam. Military planners connected to the North's political bureau constantly talked of a protracted twenty-year war.[6]

Most military operations took place in remote villages or jungle areas far from urban centers. Light-infantry battles with PAVN and PLAF troops dominated the military engagements. During the Kennedy years, the president used a counterinsurgency formula designed to separate the fish from the water.[7] The "fish" were communist guerrillas operating in the villages and hamlets of Vietnam. The "water" was the people of the rural areas in Vietnam, the bulk of the population. Military operations took the form of localized maneuvers to uproot insurgents and create pacified villages through the Strategic Hamlet Program. Kennedy's strategy met with limited success, however, and the insurgency against Ngo Dinh Diem grew at an alarming rate. In trying to isolate the insurgents, American and South Vietnamese troops precipitated an increase in their ranks. The violence in the countryside was too indiscriminate to keep neutral villagers out of the fray. Another major problem was that Diem had very little interest in the political war in the villages of South Vietnam, and the Americans were so culturally removed from Vietnamese politics that their nation-building efforts fell far short of the desired goal. It was clear by 1963 that Kennedy had to find a strategy that promised more success in the political war against the NLF. At the time of his assassination in November 1963, he was exploring his strategic options.

When Lyndon Johnson assumed the presidency following Kennedy's assassination, his inherited advisers told him that continuing along the same path in Vietnam promised few satisfactory results.[8] The president either had to get in more forcefully or get out, but the current strategy was a recipe for disaster. Ultimately, Johnson chose war. In slow and incremental steps, the president took the nation to war because he saw no other viable options. Though Johnson and his key advisers were pessimistic at times about the chances of success in Vietnam, they saw no alternative but to increase the military pressure against Hanoi. Johnson rejected the thinking of several experts who claimed that the only way to win in Vietnam was to keep military action limited and increase the political activity in Vietnam's villages.[9] After Ho had rejected Johnson's calls for a Mekong River project, the president focused more forcefully on the military half of the war, what he called the war "in cold blood."[10] Johnson eventually approved the introduction of U.S. combat troops in March 1965, coupled with the sustained bombing of North Vietnam, known as Operation Rolling Thunder.

Strategically, the United States fought a protracted war during the Johnson years (1964–1969), designed to inflict intolerable casualties on communist forces through the use of massive U.S. firepower.

Believing the war had mutated from a guerrilla conflict to large-unit warfare by 1965—and thus had shifted from a political to a military struggle—U.S. military planners hoped to crush the PAVN and the PLAF, forcing Hanoi to sue for peace. The goal was to reach the "crossover" or "breaking point" where the casualties simply became too much for the Vietnamese to accept.[11] This strategy was the brain-child of General William C. Westmoreland, whom Johnson had sent to Vietnam in 1964 as the commander of MACV (Military Assistance Command–Vietnam), which was responsible for all allied military operations in Vietnam.

There was some simple calculus involved in Westmoreland's strategy that kept U.S. military operations in line with Johnson's political and foreign policy needs. Westmoreland asked two straightforward questions: How many U.S. troops would it take to inflict significant enough casualties on the enemy to force Hanoi to surrender? And how long would it take? According to Westmoreland, it would take hundreds of thousands of U.S. troops and years, not months, to reach the crossover point.[12] He hoped the mission could be accomplished in a shorter time through employment of the other elements of grand strategy—economic and political considerations—but he was prepared to see the war of attrition through to the end.

At the heart of Westmoreland's strategy was the search-and-destroy mission. Waging what he called the "most sophisticated war in history," Westmoreland ordered U.S. troops to locate and eliminate PLAF and PAVN main infantry forces throughout South Vietnam. According to the general, "They had to be pounded with artillery and bombs and eventually brought to battle on the ground if they were not forever to remain a threat."[13] Once U.S. forces destroyed these regular units, the RVNAF could take over pacifying the guerrilla movement in the hamlets and villages of South Vietnam. Westmoreland used airpower to support forces in battle according to what some scholars have called the pile-on concept, in which U.S. troops encircled enemy units and called in the bombing raids.[14] Entire areas of South Vietnam were designated as "free fire zones," which could be attacked without regard for anyone caught in the line of fire.

The problem with Westmoreland's strategy was twofold: First, Hanoi matched each U.S. escalation of the war; second, the communists had conditioned their people to accept unusually high losses in the battle for independence and unification. PAVN infiltration into South Vietnam was crucial for victory and was completely dependent on the now-infamous Ho Chi Minh Trail. What had initially been a makeshift footpath running through eastern Laos and Cambodia to South Vietnam was transformed into a major transportation system that required hundreds of thousands of combat engineers to maintain.[15] There was also a little-known sea version of the Trail that brought men and supplies to the Cau Mau peninsula in South Vietnam.[16] Despite heavy bombing and sophisticated land mines, the United States had little impact on the flow of men and supplies from North Vietnam south. According to one Communist Party leader, the Ho Chi Minh Trail was "the lifeline of the revolution."[17] During peak times of the war, Hanoi could move over four hundred tons of supplies down the Trail each week and as many as five thousand soldiers per month.[18]

To slow this infiltration and to shore up the Saigon government, the Johnson administration also introduced a huge and sustained air

war in Vietnam. From 1960 until the 1973 Paris Peace Accords, the
United States dropped 8 million tons of bombs on the Indochina
theater.[19] That quantity represents some of the most intense bombing in history. By comparison, in all of World War II, British and U.S.
bomber forces dropped a relatively small 1.2 million tons of bombs
in all of Europe.[20] One valuable lesson from Vietnam seems to be
that it is difficult to accomplish political objectives with high-level
strategic bombing. Ironically, the Johnson and Nixon administrations
could have avoided that mistake if they had only listened to the intelligence community and the civilians in the Defense Department who
had studied the matter thoroughly.

During the Vietnam War, a number of comprehensive studies
were made to measure the effectiveness of the bombing campaign
against North Vietnam. Drawing in part on the metrics used in the
strategic-bombing studies of World War II, the Defense Department
examined the impact of the bombing on enemy morale, recruitment
for the armed services, military production, and infiltration rates.
In 1966 and 1967, a group of leading scientists under the auspices
of the JASON Division of the Institute for Defense Analyses decided that U.S. bombing had not produced the desired result. The
1967 JASON study concluded that "as of October 1967, the U.S.
bombing of North Vietnam has had no measurable effect on
Hanoi's ability to mount and support military operations in the
South." Furthermore, the report stressed that the bombing had not
even achieved the limited goal of reducing the flow of men and
supplies from north to south along the Ho Chi Minh Trail. In an
unqualified dismissal of claims of the airpower enthusiasts, the
1967 JASON study concluded:

Since the beginning of the Rolling Thunder, air strikes on NVN [North Vietnam], the flow of men and material from NVN to SVN [South Vietnam] has greatly increased, and present evidence provides no basis for concluding that the damage inflicted on North Vietnam by the bombing program has had any significant effect on this flow. In short, the flow of men and material from North Vietnam to the South appears to reflect Hanoi's intentions rather than capabilities even in the face of the bombing.[21]

Key officials at the State Department and the Central Intelligence Agency's own studies confirmed the JASON findings. Despite this pessimistic reporting, the Joint Chiefs of Staff and the U.S. military commanders in Vietnam declared the bombing had succeeded. Many policymakers and military leaders still believe this today. They argue that more bombing, not less, was needed to turn the tide in Vietnam.

This assessment looks at military strategy in a vacuum. The air war probably did more harm than good in Vietnam because it gave Hanoi a psychological edge in the important political war. One of the key aspects of Hanoi's strategy was to protract the war until U.S. policymakers lost their political will to continue the fight or until they were forced to withdraw American troops from Vietnam because the public outcry was too great. Hanoi recently announced that 3.2 million communist troops and civilians were killed during the war.[22] This huge number, when combined with RVNAF losses, represents over 10 percent of the entire population of Vietnam. That would be the equivalent today of losing to war 30 million Americans, or the entire populations of New York City, Los Angeles,

Chicago, and Boston, combined. Add to the Vietnam toll the number of Lao and Cambodian Khmer lost, and Vietnam becomes one of the deadliest wars in modern history.

The United States also suffered heavy losses in the Vietnam War. Over 58,000 U.S. service personnel were killed in Vietnam and another 150,000 were wounded.[23] The RVNAF lost over 250,000 troops.[24] These losses made it difficult for U.S. policymakers to stay the course in Vietnam, especially when Congress and large segments of the American population began to question the rationale for the war. Maintaining credibility around the globe and ensuring an independent—if not democratic—South Vietnam did not seem worth all the death and destruction. The military used massive firepower to break Hanoi's will to continue the fight, but most policy analysts today suggest the air war in Vietnam might only have strengthened the morale of North Vietnam and its citizens.[25] In South Vietnam, the air war certainly turned many friends into foes.

Although the war had reached a military stalemate in 1967, it was clear to Lyndon Johnson following the 1968 Tet Offensive that Westmoreland's protracted-war strategy was no longer viable. Despite enormous hardships and mounting casualties, the communists continued to replenish their troops. The promised "breaking point" seemed no closer in 1968 than it had in 1965, despite the huge sacrifice in American lives and funds. Much of South Vietnam had been laid to waste through American bombing missions and search-and-destroy operations. Yet there was little to show for all the death and destruction. Each American blow "was like a sledgehammer on a floating cork," reported journalist Malcolm Browne, who covered the war.[26] Accordingly, Johnson relieved Westmoreland of his command in June 1968, replacing him with General Creighton Abrams.

THE PACIFICATION STRATEGY IN VIETNAM

General Abrams altered U.S. military strategy in Vietnam immediately. Instead of relying on search-and-destroy missions that supported a protracted-war strategy, Abrams introduced the concept of pacification and a "clear-and-hold" strategy. Coupled with increased air attacks against North Vietnam, pacification and clear-and-hold promised to rid South Vietnam of its most important source of agitation, the PLAF and the NLF's political infrastructure. In short, pacification was a multifaceted program that combined incentives for NLF cadres to defect to the government's side along with targeted arrests and assassinations of the front's political leaders. In addition, U.S. troops and their RVNAF allies focused military operations on key areas in South Vietnam instead of roaming the countryside looking for communist troops. The idea was to secure villagers in South Vietnam and, at the same time, to make strategic military strikes against the communists. By 1970, pacification seemed to be a success. The South Vietnamese government controlled more territory than it had at any time since 1961, and NLF ranks had been seriously damaged.[27]

In a 2005 essay in *Foreign Affairs,* Melvin Laird, President Nixon's secretary of defense, argued that pacification had worked well in Vietnam and should be used in Iraq. He claimed that the NLF had been "largely suppressed by a combination of persuasion and force."[28] Furthermore, the success of pacification had turned the tide of the war in favor of South Vietnam. At the time of the complete U.S. withdrawal in January 1973, Laird believed the Nixon administration had left a healthy Saigon to defend itself against the communists. Pacification had changed the balance of forces in South Vietnam, and victory was all but certain. Only Soviet interference and congressional budget cuts had kept this reality from happening. Whereas Moscow was sending Hanoi more than $1 billion, the U.S. Congress had cut all funding to South Vietnam. According to Laird, without U.S. funding, "South Vietnam was quickly overrun."[29] Congress had taken away all that pacification had gained.

This is a rather optimistic view of the success of pacification. Pacification did inflict severe damage on the NLF infrastructure, but it did little to slow the PAVN. In fact, there is some evidence that the PAVN was actually standing down during the height of pacification to simply allow the United States to continue its phased withdrawal unprovoked.[30] Only after it was clear that the United States could not reengage in Vietnam did Hanoi move to its strategy of *chuyen vung,* or "upgrading the zone." This meant reclaiming territory that had been lost during the pacification program. By 1972, much of that rebuilding process had been completed. Other scholars and journalists with considerable experience in Vietnam share my assessment of pacification. David Elliott, a professor at Pomona College who spent five years in Vietnam with the U.S. Army and the Rand Corporation during the war, has concluded that optimistic reports about pacification's success are "wrong."[31] William Turley, author of the influential text *The Second Indochina War,* told a *Boston Globe* reporter that "he cannot understand why anyone would think 'clear and hold' was a success in Vietnam."[32] According to Arnold Isaacs, who covered the last three years of the Vietnam War for the *Baltimore Sun,* pacification was not the resounding success Laird has claimed it was. Isaacs noted, "A war may be going well but it isn't won if the enemy is still fighting, much less if the bloodiest battles are still to come, as Vietnam's were. And it most certainly isn't won if, when the fighting stops, the flag over the battleground—in this case the entire country of Vietnam—is the enemy's."[33]

Pacification was considerably successful against the PLAF, and evidence suggests that South Vietnam controlled more territory in 1970 than it had previously. Complicating this issue, however, is the fact that many hamlets listed as "secure" simply had been emptied as part of the U.S. program of forced-draft urbanization. Thousands of peasants had to flee to South Vietnam's cities because of the destruction of their local environments. Some U.S. analysts believed that forcing people to the cities would give the South Vietnamese government greater control over the population.[34] The thinking in Washington was that because Saigon could not effectively mobilize the rural Vietnamese, making them dependent would eliminate the need for massive political organization. Emptying the countryside fit Saigon's needs, but it also may have given a false reading on the security of South Vietnam's hamlets.

Other problems with the data also contradict the premise of pacification as a success. There have been questions about the reliability of the surveys used to determine whether the strategy of pacification was working. The basic metric used for evaluation was the Hamlet Evaluation Survey (HES), which counted the number of communists "eliminated" or "rallied" (those who joined the government) and the number of villages under South Vietnamese control. According to HES surveys, the Saigon government controlled more villages in 1971 than it had at any other time since the 1968 Tet Offensive. Some officials familiar with the HES data, however, have said HES reports were commonly inflated.[35] They have also explained that forced-draft urbanization made it difficult to examine villages. Furthermore, by 1971, the problem in South Vietnam was the increased presence of PAVN main-force infantry units. Pacification may have been a success against the PLAF, but it now seems clear that whatever losses the PAVN suffered could be replaced.

There is some merit, however, to the argument advanced by Lewis Sorley, a former U.S. Army officer with Vietnam experience who also holds a PhD from Johns Hopkins University. In his book *A Better War,* Sorley examined Abrams's policies and concluded that pacification was indeed making inroads in Vietnam, but that policymakers in Washington snatched defeat from the jaws of victory.[36] Sorley correctly analyzed that regardless of what was happening on the ground, the Nixon administration and Congress were committed to a U.S. withdrawal. Beginning in February 1970, it was official U.S. policy not to enforce a mutual withdrawal from South Vietnam.[37] PAVN troops—ten main-force infantry divisions, it turned out—were allowed to stay in South Vietnam following a unilateral U.S. troop withdrawal, because it was the only way the Nixon administration could negotiate an end to the war. Feeling domestic political pressure for that objective, the Nixon administration was negotiating in Paris a position that Sorley and many others have claimed was counter to the military reality on the ground. For Laird, Congress compounded the problem when it cut off funding for South Vietnam.

The debate over pacification will likely rage for years. Until we learn more from communist sources, it will be an argument without end. Interestingly, there are reports that many current Bush administration officials have read Sorley's book and expressed support for the ideas contained in Laird's essay.[38] Some White House voices support a pacification strategy in Iraq and see the January 2007 surge as the first phase of such a plan, and more than one Bush administration official has used the words *clear-and-hold*. Will the last phase of U.S. military involvement in Iraq include a pacification strategy and a diplomatic effort to isolate the insurgents, as was the case in Vietnam? Only time will tell, but it does seem clear that civilian military planners have made many of the same mistakes in Iraq that their predecessors did in Vietnam.

MILITARY OPERATIONS IN IRAQ

One year after the fall of Saddam Hussein, U.S. Marines found themselves in a difficult battle with insurgents in Fallujah, a small city thirty-five miles west of Baghdad. At the end of March 2004, antigovernment forces pulled four American private security contractors from their car, dismembered them, dragged them through the streets, and hung two of their bodies from a bridge over the Euphrates. The Bush White House wanted immediate revenge. With echoes of Mogadishu ringing in their ears, civilian leaders in Washington urged a swift and uncompromising response. Despite protests from U.S. commanders near Fallujah, who argued that a police action was more appropriate than a full-scale attack, the Bush administration pressed the Marines to "go in and clobber people."

On April 5, 2004, on orders from Washington, the marines launched Operation Vigilant Resolve.

What happened next transformed the Iraq War and public perceptions of the conflict. Over twenty-five hundred U.S. Marines from three battalions faced well-armed insurgents in Fallujah, and for several days the fighting was fierce. During the first days of the siege, U.S. commanders ordered the Second Battalion of the National Iraqi Army—reportedly the best in Iraq—into Fallujah but nearly a third deserted or refused the order. General James Mattis therefore asked for more U.S. troops, but he was turned down because the fighting had spread to Ramadi, Mosul, and Najaf. Not only did the Americans have to put down the insurgents, but they also had to deal with the forces of Moqtada al-Sadr, a radical Shiite cleric who controlled the Mahdi Army and whose followers made up a significant wing of the Baghdad government. With a multifront war in front of them, the marines at Fallujah counterattacked with swift and deadly air strikes. Just when it looked as if the Marines were making progress against the insurgents, the order came to launch a cease-fire and abandon the city to a loose coalition of Sunni leaders and other antigovernment forces. Apparently, some Bush officials, including Paul Bremer, who was responsible for the political side of the war, believed that a continued attack against Fallujah would destroy the fragile coalition government the United States was trying to build in Baghdad.

Watching events in Fallujah unfold, retired U.S. Marine general Anthony Zinni sighed and whispered, "I have seen this movie. It was called Vietnam." Indeed, following the debacle at Fallujah comparisons between Iraq and Vietnam were inevitable. Once again it appeared that American troops were bogged down in a protracted conflict against well-armed and highly motivated insurgents. Once again U.S. troops were giving their all to defend a national government that could not put its own army in the field at full strength. Once again policymakers in Washington had no clear-cut strategy for dealing with an asymmetrical war that required a political as well as a military program. After Fallujah, Iraq became a state of mind, just like Vietnam three decades earlier. Only one year after the invasion of Iraq, many Americans wondered if this conflict was worth more U.S. blood and treasure. Despite these misgivings, the Bush administration seemed intent on turning a political disaster in Baghdad into a regional security catastrophe.

At the core of the thinking on Iraq following the Fallujah debacle was the belief the war against the insurgents must come first on a list of high priorities. Following Fallujah American troops conducted numerous raids into hostile areas, hoping to arrest insurgents and gain intelligence to cripple the antigovernment movement. The idea was also to kill as many insurgents as possible and, at the same time, provide security to the Iraqi people. This was a difficult balance to strike. As car bombings increased, it became more difficult for U.S. forces to focus on the political war. The war took on a distinctly urban flavor. Insurgents took cabs to their target areas and escaped the same way. Leaders of the insurgency spent most of their days driving to remote areas of Iraq, just ahead of U.S. forces in armored personnel carriers. The car bomb came to symbolize the war in Iraq largely because the road was the war's most significant center of gravity.[39] Night goggles and infrared sensors meant U.S. troops owned the night, and they used this advantage to strike at the heart of the insurgency. In the daytime, U.S. soldiers joined their coalition allies in armored convoys to locate insurgent bases and destroy them.

The battle against Iraqi insurgents took some strange twists and turns, beginning with national elections in January 2005. On January 30, 2005, an estimated 8 million Iraqis voted in elections for a transitional National Assembly. The Shia United Iraqi Alliance won a majority of assembly seats, and combined Kurdish parties came in second. Sunni representatives were few in number. Within one month of the election, a car bomb in Hilla, a city just south of Baghdad, killed 114 people, the worst single incident since the U.S.-led invasion. That spring, following the bombing at Hilla and the selection of Jalal Talabani, a Kurd, as president of Iraq and Ibraham Jaafri, a Shia, as prime minister, the sectarian violence intensified dramatically. In May 2005, the number of civilian deaths due to car bombs, explosions, and assassination doubled from the previous month. By July 2005, over 25,000 Iraqi civilians had been killed since the March 2003 invasion. Most of the violence was between Sunni insurgents and Shia connected to various political and military alliances. When the Shia-led United Iraqi Alliance emerged as the winner of the December 2005 parliamentary elections, insurgent attacks threatened to destabilize the Baghdad government even more.

The sectarian violence in Iraq intensified dramatically in February 2006 following the bombing of an important Shia shrine in Samarra. In the next six months, attacks and counterattacks wreaked havoc in Sunni and Shia neighborhoods all over Iraq. In May and June 2006, the United Nations reported that at least 100 civilians were being killed each day.[40] Many policymakers in Washington hoped that the newly appointed prime minister, Jawad al-Maliki, would bring Sunnis, Kurds, and Shia together in the new coalition government in Baghdad. However, Maliki failed to distance himself from some of the more radical elements of the Shia power establishment, including Moqtada al-Sadr, and the violence raged out of control. After Saddam Hussein's trial and eventual execution in late 2006, Sunni reprisal attacks in Shia neighborhoods were a common occurrence. In November 2006, a car bombing in the mostly Shia neighborhood of Sadr City in Baghdad killed 213 and set off a new wave of attacks against the insurgents.

Under General George Casey, who was commander of U.S. ground forces in Iraq from June 2004 to February 2007, much emphasis was given to a limited clear-and-hold pacification strategy. He believed that a limited number of U.S. troops could provide the basic counterinsurgency program in Iraq, while American advisers trained the National Iraqi Army for the bulk of the military operations. General Casey believed that targeted strikes against insurgents held out the best hope for political gain in Baghdad and could, in fact, keep the civil war in Iraq limited. In retrospect, his undying belief in the government's ability to build a coalition in Baghdad and in the National Iraqi Army to provide security was shortsighted. The violence in Iraq actually intensified dramatically in the Casey years. The primary problem was that insurgents continued to create a threat environment that forced U.S. troops away from street patrols and light-infantry maneuvers, separating the Americans from Iraqi civilians and the political war (winning hearts and minds). In asymmetrical wars, insurgents depend on the larger power's backing away from political objectives. By keeping the pressure on, insurgent groups hoped to destabilize the government to the point of forcing an American withdrawal.

President Bush supported the Casey strategy, as did Secretary of Defense Donald Rumsfeld. The Bush administration often stated that the development of Iraqi security forces was a key component for success in the war. The president was fond of saying, "Our strategy can be summed up this way: As the Iraqis stand up, we will stand down." Critics of this policy, such as Andrew Krepenevich, an expert on the army in Vietnam, argued that the president and General Casey were describing a withdrawal plan, but not a political and military strategy.[41] Furthermore, Casey's emphasis on killing insurgents while ignoring the political program proved to be a major mistake. Piling up dead bodies without any political program to move civil society forward in Iraq was a recipe for disaster. In the absence of political progress, the increased violence that was needed to stop insurgent attacks actually turned much of the population away from American goals. Indeed, by late 2006, the Casey strategy had failed to produce significant progress on the military or political front, and therefore, the Bush administration decided to replace him with General David H. Petraeus. General Petraeus was a longtime advocate of increased U.S. troops in Iraq and of a focus on a larger pacification program and nation building.

THE SURGE AND IRAQI SECURITY

When General Petraeus assumed command of all U.S. forces in Iraq in February 2007, he introduced what is now known as the surge, an increase of thirty thousand U.S. troops to put down the insurgency and bring stability to Baghdad. The surge included an intensification of the pacification program, with the goal of clearing out insurgents in some Baghdad neighborhoods and in Anbar province. U.S. troops would then stay in these cleared areas, hoping to quell the violence by providing round-the-clock security in districts where death squads had once roamed.[42] The program also included an enticement, in some cases arms and in other cases money, for Sunni insurgents in Anbar province not to attack U.S. convoys or Iraqi government troops. By all initial reports, the surge has reduced attacks in Iraq significantly. Still, several factors could undermine the surge's success.

Complicating the battle against the insurgency in Iraq is Moqtada al-Sadr and his Mahdi Army. Al-Sadr is a powerful figure inside Iraq, and his family has hard-won political support from many Iraqis for suffering firsthand at the hands of Saddam Hussein. Shiites who stood in strong opposition to Hussein, like al-Sadr's family, hold key positions in the new Iraqi government. In fact, Iraqi prime minister al-Maliki owes his political fortunes to al-Sadr and his supporters. However, the Mahdi Army has responded to Sunni attacks against Shiite shrines and in Shiite neighborhoods with brute force and outside the military chain of command of the National Iraqi Army. Acting as an independent agent, yet with strong ties to the government, al-Sadr and his army always present the United States with difficult policy decisions. Some Washington officials support cutting all ties with al-Sadr, yet others believe he sits atop a legitimate political movement in Iraq, no matter how distasteful he may be personally.

Over 2007 and into 2008, al-Sadr did seem to have modified his views about attacks in Sunni neighborhoods. He has agreed to a cease-fire twice since the announcement of the surge, the second promise extending all the way to August 2008. The problem is that some radical Shiites, such as Abdul Aziz al-Hakim, believe al-Sadr has sold out their cause and vow to renew violence against Sunnis. If this happens, it may be impossible to begin a phased U.S. troop withdrawal in the summer of 2008, as promised by the Bush administration to gain support for the surge. In other words, the surge—which was to pave the way for an American troop withdrawal—may, in fact, take on a more permanent status. Secretary of Defense Robert Gates, who replaced Rumsfeld in December 2006, has called this new development the "pause." He suggests that significant progress has been made in Iraq, but that further evaluation is needed before more American troops can be brought home. For many radical Shiites and some Sunni leaders, the pause is simply a euphemism for a long-term U.S. occupation.

Despite these obstacles, many observers believe the infusion of U.S. troops has made all the difference and Iraq is more secure and moving forward with its political program. Supporters of the surge believe this kind of progress was possible all along if former secretary of defense Donald Rumsfeld had only introduced more U.S. troops sooner. Others believe combined U.S. and Iraqi forces now have the resources needed to capture rebel strongholds and hold onto them. According to two Iraqi bloggers with a large following in the United States, Mohammed and Omar Fadhil, the new surge resembles the old clear-and-hold strategy employed by General Abrams in Vietnam. People in Baghdad, they claim, have been waiting for the United States to commit the resources needed for the "hold" to materialize. The plan to secure Baghdad, according to the Fadhils, is "becoming stricter and gaining momentum by the day as more troops pour into the city, allowing for better implementation of the 'clear and hold' strategy."[43]

Others have suggested that the surge's initial victory was psychological. Enemies of the Baghdad government went into hiding, believing additional U.S. troops made it impossible for their militant groups to operate freely. The number of security tips about insurgent operations increased dramatically following the surge, and stores and marketplaces have reopened all over Baghdad. Some journalists have seen dramatic differences in Iraq between their tours. NBC's Brian Williams, for example, reported in early 2007 that there had been dramatic changes in Ramadi since his previous visit there one year earlier.[44] Still, the surge has not significantly altered the political or military landscape in Iraq. The overemphasis on killing insurgents in the early years of the war, coupled with an inexplicable reluctance on the part of the Bush administration to build a meaningful political program into its nation-building efforts in Iraq, has saddled the current U.S. command with intractable problems. No matter how effective the surge is, or how much better General Petraeus's strategy is than his predecessor's, Iraq remains a damaged state.

Furthermore, there is a growing feeling among many U.S. policymakers that the Baghdad government has seen the surge and General Petraeus's accounting of it as mechanisms to simply buy more time for their own agendas to play out. As Thomas Friedman of the *New York Times* pointed out in fall 2007, few in Baghdad act out of anything other than self-interest. According to Friedman, Iraqi leaders continue to "look out for themselves, their clans, their hometowns, their militias and their sects," and they also use the Iraqi treasury and ministries "as looting grounds for personal or sectarian gains."[45] Indeed, there is some evidence that Iraqi leaders are not spending much time together discussing military and political strategy. On the contrary, most seem content to simply wait for the United States to leave Iraq before starting the real civil war. And there is some evidence that some Sunnis have renewed attacks against Shia neighborhoods in what can only be described as a Sunni awakening following the surge. The problem for U.S. policymakers all along has been that no strategy in Iraq has been able to consolidate whatever gains have been made militarily. Early in the war, civilians in the Pentagon placed too much emphasis on killing insurgents, and even after Rumsfeld's departure, there has been too little progress in the political war.

The United States failed to win the hearts and minds of the peasants in Vietnam, and the same problem remains the most significant obstacle to success in Iraq. A senior U.S. Army commander in Baghdad reported early in the war that he did not see the attempt to win hearts and minds in Iraq as "one of the metrics of success."[46] Thankfully, that attitude has changed with General Petraeus's arrival in Baghdad. The political war is vital to success in Iraq, however defined. Following the invasion of Iraq, the feeling among many in Washington was that the United States had to "fix" Iraq because Americans had "broken it."[47] The insurgency is only part of the problem in Iraq. As was true in Vietnam, winning the support of the population is more important to the long-term success of the government than killing insurgents. And the key to the political war may, in fact, be the ability to separate the various insurgent groups and their objectives. The Bush administration's dogged insistence that the insurgency in Iraq is uncomplicated—that it is simply international terrorists at work—is the major obstacle to long-term success in the counterinsurgency program and nation building. The first rule of war is to know your enemy. The Bush administration failed that test from day one.

THE NATIONAL LIBERATION FRONT

Knowing the enemy in Vietnam was also essential to the war's conduct and outcome. Throughout the Vietnam War, the NLF was at the center of key political and military operations. The front was completely homegrown and possessed a very specific military and political agenda. Born in December 1960 in the mangrove swamps of Tay Ninh province, near Vietnam's border with Cambodia, the NLF, derogatorily known in the West as the Viet Cong, was a classical communist front organization. After six years of trying to liberate South Vietnam through political means alone, the Vietnamese Communist Party had finally decided that the time had come to overthrow Ngo Dinh Diem, South Vietnam's first president, by force. To accomplish this goal, the party approved the formation of a broad-based united front "to rally all patriotic classes and sections of the people . . . to oppose the U.S.-Diem regime."[48] The NLF was directly under the control of the party's central committee, but it worked tirelessly to recruit noncommunists to its cause. Political cadres were active in urban areas, Diem's only base of support, and of course, the NLF was interested in winning over the rural areas.

In the early years of the war, the NLF's insurgency relied on a combination of political and military struggle movements to enlist cadres. Its goals, as stated in a captured party document, were to "lessen enemy pressure, oppose military operations and terrorism, oppose the strategic hamlet program, and halt the seizure of land and the corvee labor system [conscripted unpaid workers]."[49] To accomplish these objectives, the NLF engaged in a people's war in villages throughout South Vietnam. A concept borrowed in part from the Chinese communists, a people's war stresses the political nature of a military struggle.

In practice, the people's war in Vietnam relied heavily on the NLF cadres' ability to communicate the ideas of the revolution to a war-ravaged rural population in South Vietnam. According to one of the most important Communist Party publications on the village war, "Needs of the Revolution," NLF cadres should "choose the right moment to act . . . when the people's rights have been endangered." The NLF political leadership defined these threats as "corruption, high taxation, forced money donations, land robbing, military draft." After these conditions had been identified, party leaders explained, "struggle movements can then be launched in favor of freedom of travel, freedom to work, freedom of trade, freedom to move to a new part of the country, and for village council elections."[50] Cadres used this technique to convince villagers that they represented the vanguard of a new social movement that would return control of their hamlets to them. In response to this political message, NLF cadre ranks swelled by nearly 300 percent a month during the first year.[51]

Of course, there was a military side to the insurgency as well. In the early years of the NLF, the insurgency used terror to send a message to Diem and his supporters that they could no longer have their way in South Vietnam.[52] Car bombs, convoy ambushes, night raids on villages, and political assassinations were common insurgent activities. By late 1961, however, the insurgency was regularized in the sense that the NLF had formed several main-force infantry divisions that received significant material and technical support from Hanoi. Although the concept of the people's war remained in place, insurgents now practiced more conventional forms of warfare. Nowhere was this shift more apparent than at the battle of Ap Bac in January 1963, where the PLAF's 261st Main-Force Battalion shot down five U.S. helicopters and killed sixty RVNAF soldiers while suffering only minor losses.[53]

In the early years of the war, President Kennedy feared the growing insurgency in Vietnam as much as any cold war problem. To deal with the NLF, he quickly developed counterinsurgency measures in Vietnam based on the British experience in Malaya.[54] Instead of sending in U.S. combat troops, Kennedy created strategic hamlets, designed to isolate the NLF from the peasants by building new, protected hamlets. American advisers relocated villagers to these newly constructed safe havens to separate them from the communists and facilitate South Vietnam's social programs. The goal, according to counterinsurgency expert Roger Hilsman, was to reduce NLF cadres to "hungry, marauding bands of outlaws devoting all their energies to remaining alive."[55] Of course, the United States and its South Vietnamese allies experienced little success against the insurgency in the early years of the war. Only after the battles became more conventional, and the insurgency gave way to coordinated attacks of the North Vietnam's People's Army, did the United States experience any military success.

The NLF's relationship to the communists in Hanoi was complex, and at times strained. Although the NLF was a classical communist front, there were regional differences within Vietnam's

Communist Party. During the early years of the war, 1955–1960, northern members of the party did not want to launch all-out military attacks against Diem and South Vietnam.[56] Instead, they hoped to regroup from heavy losses suffered in the war that had just ended with the French and to reunite Vietnam through political means alone. Some northerners even held out the promise that the elections called for in the 1954 Geneva Accords would take place, and that Ho Chi Minh, president of Vietnam's Communist Party, would take his rightful place as the leader of a united Vietnam. Political leaders in Hanoi were also careful to follow the wishes of their allies in Moscow and Beijing. Both China and the Soviet Union supported the political struggle against "imperialism" in Vietnam in the mid to late 1950s, fearing that the United States might once again intervene in the region if Ho Chi Minh launched a military struggle against his rivals inside Vietnam. Still smarting from the Korean War, neither socialist superpower wanted to provoke the United States into any action that might threaten the regional balance of power.

The South Vietnamese communists believed that their northern counterparts should support a more vigorous armed struggle against Diem, no matter what Hanoi's benefactors wanted. They constantly pushed for a more active military stance in South Vietnam and, in 1959, even launched insurgent attacks against Diem's forces without Hanoi's approval. Ultimately, party leaders in Hanoi had to approve military action or risk losing control of the insurgency in South Vietnam.[57] The creation of the NLF, therefore, was a way for the party to gain more influence over the insurgency and its political and military operations. U.S. intelligence officers stationed in Vietnam recognized the relationship between Hanoi and the NLF soon after the NLF's formation, but they had a difficult job convincing Washington that the insurgency was not a cross-border invasion.

From the earliest days of the Vietnam War, key members of the Kennedy administration claimed that Saigon was under attack by communist forces originating in North Vietnam. The United States supported this claim with several White House position papers concluding that communist North Vietnam was trying to take an independent and democratic South Vietnam by force.[58] Washington also developed a doctrine to reflect that perception. U.S. military officials first assigned to Vietnam believed any attack against South Vietnam would come from the north. The thinking among American leaders in Washington and Saigon reflected the previous U.S. combat experience in Korea. The general outlook of U.S. Army doctrine was that revolution could not be instigated or successful without the support of an external sponsoring power.[59] The U.S. experience in Korea suggested that the guerrillas now operating freely in South Vietnam were the early warning of cross-border conventional attacks, far more serious than any local insurgency.[60]

U.S. officials now know, however, that the NLF insurgency was made up exclusively of southerners. In fact, even after the NLF's formation in 1960, Hanoi was reluctant to send main-force infantry units south to support the insurgency. Only at the Vietnamese Communist Party's ninth plenum in December 1963 did the party's political bureau agree to aid the southern revolution with arms and men.[61] Following that decision, it took nearly two years for these approved troops and supplies to make their way south down the Ho Chi Minh Trail. These troops arrived just in time for the now-infamous battle of the Ia Drang Valley.

The American misreading of the character of the NLF allowed the communists to take advantage of the growing credibility gap between Washington and the American public. The NLF exploited this situation by creating a Foreign Relations Commission that routinely published position papers claiming independence from Hanoi and no ties to China or the Soviet Union. NLF leaders repeated these claims in meetings with many world leaders and others in Vietnam, Europe, Canada, and even the United States.[62] By 1965 and the introduction of American ground troops into Vietnam, few believed that the NLF was controlled by Hanoi. The result was a devastating impact on U.S. policy that placed Washington and its Saigon allies in a reactive position. The NLF was heralded around the globe as freedom fighters akin to the minutemen at Lexington and Concord. Any move Washington made, therefore, was seen not against the ideological backdrop of the cold war, but rather as a superpower fighting against patriotic peasants. The NLF's larger connections to the communist world were never part of the public debate. Washington never fully recovered from its initial mistake, even though U.S. intelligence officers in Vietnam understood the insurgency quite well by 1962. The propaganda and political advantage had gone to Hanoi and its supporters in the NLF.

WHO LEADS THE INSURGENCY IN IRAQ?

In Iraq today the insurgents and their goals remain a mystery. By most accounts, the important insurgency groups in Iraq are Sunnis connected to the Iraqi Islamic Army and former Baathists connected to Saddam's regime. These Sunni groups are joined occasionally by foreign jihadist groups working with Osama bin Laden, such as Ansar al-Islam. In 2005, al-Qaeda in Iraq joined the fighting. While all oppose the U.S. presence in Iraq, it is difficult to gauge their interests beyond a desire for a U.S. withdrawal and war against the Shiite majority. Some insurgent groups support pan-Arab nationalism. Others want a theocracy in Iraq. They cling to the idea of a Taliban-like Islamic government coming to power and promoting Islamic revolution throughout the region. Taken together, the various insurgent groups seem focused more on toppling the existing Iraqi government and embarrassing the United States than on offering a clear political alternative. What the insurgents oppose is clear, but what they support is not. The insurgents in Iraq do not have a carefully translated ten-point program like the National Liberation Front's in Vietnam.[63] That we do not know more about the insurgency speaks volumes. It seems clear that intelligence failures have been a key factor in the war in Iraq all along.

At this point, violence seems to be the only unifying factor in the Iraqi insurgency. For the core of Sunni insurgents, any individual, group, or organization willing to use violence against the occupation is seen as a potential ally, though there have been problems between some Sunni groups and al-Qaeda in Iraq. In late December 2007, there were signs that the insurgency was turning on itself. Reports that al-Qaeda fighters were the target of Iraqi insurgent strikes suggest that anti-Americanism might not be enough to unite the disparate groups in Iraq. Still, it is quite possible that trained jihadists can gain control of the insurgency inside Iraq and turn Iraq into another Afghanistan—where the government has nominal control of the population—once U.S. troops are forced to withdraw. One

favored tactic of the insurgents is to attack civilian populations nom-
inally under U.S. control. This violence is designed to increase U.S.
casualties and also to show ordinary Iraqis that their allies cannot
protect them. The overall goal is to force the United States to leave
Iraq before the new government can solidify its control of the country. Breaking Iraqi confidence in the United States is the cornerstone
of that program.

Although this tactic has met with some success, the Iraqi insurgency still lacks a unifying agenda other than anti-Americanism and
war against Shiites. No single leader or organization has galvanized
the opposition parties in Iraq, and it is unlikely that the world will
see an Iraqi version of Ho Chi Minh step forward to represent the insurgents' political goals. The only discernible endgame for the insurgents is their angry reaction to events in Iraq. The idea of three
separate states—one Kurdish, one Sunni, and one Shiite—may be a
long-term goal, but the political and military complications associated with such aspirations cannot fuel insurgent fires for long. Without the national leadership projected by a charismatic figure, the
insurgents have alienated large segments of the population with
their indiscriminate attacks on civilian targets. All the cold war's
most radical leaders had a political agenda that fueled their revolutionary ideology. The world knew what Mao, Guevara, Castro, and
Ho stood for in the cold war and knew how they hoped to accomplish their political goals. In Iraq, the insurgents lack any proactive
political agenda other than separation and revenge.

Some supporters of the insurgency in Iraq have suggested that it
is premature for one group to dominate the political direction of the

anti-American movement. They argue that the Iraqi insurgency is much like China's united-front strategy in the 1930s or Vietnam's NLF during the 1960s.[64] This is a serious misreading of history. The united front in Asian communist movements always made temporary alliances with potential enemies as long as they supported the revolution's overall goals, but at no time did the Communist Party relinquish control of the insurgency or its political and military movements. In China and Vietnam, the revolution's main objective was to replace one social system with another. The party offered a clear political alternative to the government in power. In Iraq, the various insurgent groups have not followed the same path. This is not a people's war. Its only unifying theme seems to be the old Bolshevik adage "The worse, the better."

Despite the lack of unifying message or national political ideology delivered by a charismatic leader, the Iraqi insurgency continues to present the United States with a number of difficult problems. Increasing attacks on civilian targets have prompted U.S. military commanders in Iraq to launch more anti-insurgent patrols. This strategy gives American forces a target, but it also reinforces the notion that the United States is an occupying force, or the power that harms Islam. Much like the British in Ireland during "the troubles," the United States finds itself patrolling vast stretches of Iraq behind heavy armor. American patrols have now focused on many areas in the Red Zone—the generally unsecured provinces of Anbar, Nineveh, and Salah ad Din—the heart of the insurgency. Missions in the Red Zone have left the Green Zone—the heavily fortified area inside Baghdad—open to insurgent attacks. The insurgents, no doubt, understand that attacks against civilians in the Green Zone shake the confidence of ordinary Iraqis, and as a result, these attacks intensified in late 2007 and early 2008.

Despite the insurgency's limited success, the problem for the Bush administration in Iraq has never been the performance of the U.S. military. American troops have done everything asked of them. Rather, the problem has always been that massive U.S. military power has no political corollary. The fundamental problem in Iraq is political: How does the United States win the hearts and minds of ordinary Iraqis? How does the United States increase the viability of the government in Baghdad? Can Iraqi security forces provide the context for the Iraqi government's political agenda—if it has one—to take root? Answers to all of these questions rest on the ability of the United States to have more success in nation building in Iraq than it did in Vietnam.

CHAPTER THREE

THE PROBLEMS OF NATION BUILDING

D URING A presidential debate with Vice President Al Gore in 2000, then presidential candidate George W. Bush declared, "I don't think our troops ought to be used for what's called nation building."[1] Eight years later, the biggest problem facing the United States in Iraq is building a stable government in Baghdad. It will remain so for years to come for several reasons, not the least of which is that the Bush administration made absolutely no plans for post–Saddam Hussein Iraq. The Bush team believed it could quickly turn its limited invasion force into peacekeepers without addressing fundamental social, economic, and political problems in Iraq. It also believed that democracy alone would transform Baghdad and offer a stellar example for the rest of the Middle East. The Bush administration dismissed the hard-learned lesson from Vietnam that socioeconomic progress and social justice should be the cornerstone of civil society. Only recently has the Bush White House moved away from its massive privatization efforts in Iraq to focus more on the well-being of ordinary Iraqis.

Because the Bush administration took to nation building so hesi-
tantly, the president admitted in early 2008 that there are still significant problems to overcome before more U.S. troops can come
home. Increasingly, President Bush is putting the burden of success
on the Iraqis themselves, at the same time refusing to acknowledge
his administration's role in the political failures in Iraq. No one
wants a failed state in the Middle East, but the Bush administration
seemed intent on creating one by refusing to engage in a serious study
of post-Hussein Iraq. Most reliable intelligence experts predicted a
clash between Sunnis, Kurds, and Shia following the overthrow of
Saddam Hussein. Yet, in a move reminiscent of the Vietnam War,
the Bush administration charged full blast up a dead-end alley in Iraq
with little regard for Iraqi political culture or history. Grandiose
ideas about democracy promotion are no substitute for sound political judgment and action. Iraq's fragile coalition of Kurds, Sunnis,
and Shiites has a troubled history, but few in the Bush administration bothered to notice.

In the absence of a meaningful political plan in Iraq, Congress has
recently—although belatedly—required the president to push the
Iraqi government to move forward with constitutional protections
and a more inclusive agenda. It has also demanded a better accounting from the Bush administration on progress in Iraq. The new
Democratic leadership is trying to make its mark with the White
House and its constituents by taking a stand against the war. As of
mid–2008, that effort has failed to produce any immediately binding
resolutions to bring American troops home or to limit U.S. spending
in Iraq. What Congress did do, however, was to include benchmarks

for the Iraqi government in its legislation authorizing the president's plan to send thirty thousand more U.S. troops to Iraq as part of the surge strategy. President Bush eventually signed this legislation in May 2007. A strict requirement for congressional support, therefore, was a series of midyear assessments on Iraq. The first came in July 2007. The White House reported that significant progress had been made on a number of fronts, but that it was too soon after the surge to measure its impact on the political situation inside Iraq. When General Petraeus and U.S. ambassador to Iraq Ryan Crocker gave their required reports to Congress in September 2007, it was clear that congressional leaders thought nation building had failed.

According to the Government Accountability Office (GAO), which had been charged with measuring progress on the congressional benchmarks, the Baghdad government failed to meet fifteen of the eighteen U.S. targets. The overly optimistic reporting of the Bush administration had given way to one failure after another in Baghdad. Especially alarming was a State Department report claiming that religious freedom in Iraq had deteriorated sharply during the past year. Many members of Congress believed that this measuring stick was most significant because it tested the Baghdad government's ability and willingness to bring Sunnis and Kurds into national political life. Furthermore, the Bush White House, following public debate about the negative GAO report, downplayed the importance of the benchmarks and of political progress in Iraq, claiming that the Iraqis face many difficulties and should not be on a U.S. timetable. This administration simply does not understand the complexities of nation building in Iraq, and this has been the problem all along.

THE FUTURE OF IRAQ PROJECT

Indeed, the problems of nation building in Iraq were present before the March 2003 invasion. It now seems clear the Bush administration purposefully ignored the available expertise on Iraq, sources that might have helped in its nation-building program.[2] According to Paul Pillar, a national intelligence officer on the Middle East (2000–2005), the Bush administration persistently overlooked U.S. intelligence on the efficacy of a war in Iraq and the problems of nation building there in order to pursue its larger agenda of democracy promotion. In a 2006 essay in *Foreign Affairs*, Pillar concluded that the intelligence community had sent the administration a message prior to the 2003 invasion specifying that sanctions against Saddam Hussein promised the best success and that there was no pressing reason to go to war. Furthermore, the intelligence community had warned the Bush administration that if the United States did go to war, it must "prepare for a messy aftermath."[3] In fact, the administration not only ignored the intelligence community on these pressing matters but also turned its back on experts that it had gathered to focus on the problems in Iraq.

From the earliest stages of the planning for war, the administration was inclined to ignore the recommendations of the Future of Iraq Project, a group assembled by the U.S. State Department in early 2002 to help plan for a post-Saddam Iraq. The group included Iraqi exiles, experts from the State Department's Middle East Bureau, economists, security specialists, and political consultants. They met in a series of topical workshops designed to give the Bush administration the best thinking on nation building after the potential overthrow of Saddam Hussein. The project issued a number of specific reports, especially on the social aspects of nation building.

Shortly before the invasion of Iraq, however, the Pentagon took full control of the Project, rejecting much of the already completed work. According to retired U.S. general Jay Garner, who took over the Project at the Pentagon, former secretary of defense Donald Rumsfeld had told him to "shelve" the Future of Iraq Project.[4] There had been significant debate between the State Department and the Pentagon over the Project, but on the eve of the invasion, the Bush administration made the calculated decision to scrap the Project in favor of its own military planners and what would become the Office for Reconstruction and Humanitarian Assistance (ORHA). Instead of focusing on the social and economic aspects of nation building, General Garner and ORHA focused almost entirely on promoting democracy. For some, like Richard Perle, the former chairman of the Defense Policy Board, an influential group of advisers to the Pentagon, and Kanan Makiya, an Iraqi intellectual and adviser to the Iraqi National Congress, the ORHA corrected much of the State Department's flawed thinking on nation building. According to Makiya, the State Department was interested only in meaningless social questions, such as how the United States could collect garbage in the streets the day after Iraqi liberation, or how Americans could recruit health care workers.[5]

For Perle and Makiya, the real problems were political. They were more interested in "big picture questions."[6] Perle has suggested that the State Department stood in the way of the Bush administration's plans for meaningful change in Iraq. He has argued repeatedly that the State Department and the CIA refused to engage Iraqis about the composition of the post-Saddam government and the transition to democracy. According to Perle, nation building would have been very successful in Iraq if the State Department had not been so parochial about what could be accomplished.[7] For Makiya, the State Department and the CIA were the biggest enemies of democracy in Iraq.[8] He was relieved, as was Perle, when the Defense Department took over the planning effort, and he believed that Paul Bremer and his colleagues at the Coalition Provisional Authority (CPA) made up for lost time and missed opportunities. In retrospect, the Bremer-led CPA created more problems than it solved in Iraq and remains responsible for much of the political chaos in Baghdad today.

THE RAND REPORT

Bremer followed through on many of General Garner's postwar plans but also introduced some new democracy programs supported by the Bush administration. As head of the CPA, Bremer endorsed a Rand Corporation report titled "America's Role in Nation-Building: From Germany to Iraq."[9] Bremer called the study "a marvelous how-to manual for post-conflict stabilization and reconstruction." Furthermore, he declared, "I have kept a copy handy since my arrival in Baghdad and recommend it to anyone who wishes to understand or engage in such activities."[10] Bremer's colleagues in the Pentagon were equally impressed by the Rand report and followed many of its recommendations for postwar Iraq. For most Bush administration officials, whatever problems may have existed in planning and execution prior to Bremer's arrival in Baghdad were fixed by close adherence to the recommendations in the Rand study. Bremer's replacement, John Negroponte, also followed the Rand blueprint for success.

The Rand study called for sweeping changes in the political, economic, and security structures in Iraq. It suggested that the Bush administration take advantage of Iraq's existing nationwide civil administration, use the United Nations to help with humanitarian problems, and use Iraq's oil reserves to reduce Baghdad's dependence on foreign aid. The study also warned that the United States cannot "afford to contemplate early exit strategies or leave the job half completed. The real question should not be how soon it can leave, but how fast and how much to share power with Iraqis and the international community while retaining enough power to oversee an enduring transition to democracy."[11] Rand also suggested that the United States mend its rift with its European allies because the nation-building project in Iraq would require multilateral action and cost sharing.[12]

What the Rand study does not mention, however, is Vietnam. Instead, it uses case studies from U.S. nation-building efforts in Germany, Japan, Somalia, Haiti, Bosnia, Kosovo, and Afghanistan. A footnote to the study suggests that Vietnam was a "status quo" war, and that the U.S. nation-building effort was "too short" and "too limited" in its political objectives to warrant study.[13] Obviously, today's Rand researchers have forgotten that the Rand Corporation was at the very center of America's twenty-year effort at nation building in Vietnam. The Vietnam War was in many ways all about providing a stable government in Saigon as a counterrevolutionary alternative to Ho Chi Minh's communists. The entire war rested on the viability of the Saigon government and its ability to convince its people that it was a legitimate, sovereign state. This is precisely what the Bush administration now faces in Iraq as it tries to convince Sunnis, Shiites, and Kurds to give up their separate political agendas for a unified, national one.

WHAT IS A NATION?

At the heart of any nation-building effort is redefining for the citizens what it means to belong to a nation. Scholars have been engaged in this exercise for decades, and some social-scientific reading is essential to an understanding of how to reconstruct Iraq. More than a decade ago, historian Benedict Anderson noted that nations are not natural but "imagined communities" requiring a great deal of blind faith. To him, the creation of nations is often a purely cognitive undertaking. Common languages, customs, and history are often imagined or constructed by civilians to purposely strengthen bonds for survival.[14] Eric Hobsbawm picked up on Anderson's theme, suggesting that most traditions that unite disparate people into a nation are invented.[15] To Ernest Renan, the nation is a "large-scale solidarity, constituted by the feeling of the sacrifices that one has made in the past and those that one is prepared to make in the future." He concluded, however, that the single variable that ties people to a nation is the "desire to continue a common life."[16]

Michael Howard took a different approach. For Howard, the principle of nationalism has always been "indissolubly linked, both in theory and practise, with the idea of war."[17] Barbara Ehrenreich agreed. In her book *Blood Rites: Origins and History of the Passions of War*, Ehrenreich argued that the nation is "our imagined link to the glorious deeds—or the terrible atrocities still awaiting revenge—that were performed by others long ago." Her conclusion is that the nation is "a warrior lineage in which everyone can now claim membership."[18]

If past sacrifice and a desire to share a common future are at the crux of nationhood, it is no wonder that the Bush administration is having such a difficult time in Iraq. Ethnic, tribal, religious, social, and political divisions are the hallmark of modern Iraqi history. It now seems clear that Saddam Hussein held these disparate groups together only by brute force. Complicating matters for the Bush administration is the way that Iraq became a modern nation-state. As historian Niall Ferguson and others have suggested, the Bush administration's difficulties today in nation building have their roots in the British experience in Iraq in the early twentieth century.[19] In 1914, when the British discovered Turkey was entering World War I on the side of the Germans, Prime Minister Lloyd George supported incursions into Iraq to secure key strategic areas for the British. General Charles Townshend launched a series of military raids into southern Iraq but failed in his initial attempts to take Baghdad. After two years of heavy fighting, the British finally captured the city. Arab allies connected with Husayn ibn Ali (the sharif of Mecca) led a revolt against the Ottoman Turks, helping Britain secure victory. At the end of the war, Britain established a new monarchy under the leadership of Ali's son, Prince Fayisal. Britain then defined the national boundaries of Iraq, with little regard for natural land constraints or traditional tribal and ethnic settlements, and this postwar policy produced the merger of Sunnis, Kurds, and Shiites into a modern Iraqi state. Now that Saddam is gone, the trick is how to hold these disparate groups together and to convince them that a future in common is in their best interest.

In Vietnam, in sharp contrast, the idea of nationhood held almost mythical qualities. Ho Chi Minh was fond of saying that Vietnam was "one nation and one people with four thousand years of history."[20] Although Ho seriously overstated the case, Vietnam has indeed had a long romance with its national history. Founded by migrating tribes from southern China, Vietnam has had a dependent but resistant cultural, social, and political relationship with its powerful northern neighbor. Throughout centuries of contact, Vietnam adopted many Chinese institutions and cultural and political habits, but it also created its own. Several independence movements depended upon the construction of an identity free of Chinese influence. In 40 CE, the Trung sisters avenged the death of a relative at Chinese hands by establishing the first independence movement in Vietnam. Although the Chinese quelled the rebellion three years later, the Trung sisters are still celebrated today in Vietnam as the founders of a nationalistic independence movement dating back two thousand years. Their images can be seen throughout Vietnam, and one of the busiest streets in Hanoi still carries their name, Hai Ba Trung.

In the fifteenth century, Vietnam gained its full independence from China in a series of battles that now incorporate the country's most important national myth. In 1428, Le Loi, a wealthy landowner, led a revolt against the Ming occupation. Unsure of how to defeat his more powerful rivals, Le Loi went to a lake in the center of Hanoi to search for an answer. A tortoise came to him with a magical sword that could be used to defeat the Chinese only if it were returned to the lake. Le Loi took the sword, defeated the Ming overlords, and returned the sword to the lake. That lake now bears the name Lake of the Restored Sword, and Le Loi is one of Vietnam's most celebrated national heroes, ascending to the throne as Emperor Le Thai To. For nearly four hundred years, the later Le dynasty ruled Vietnam, recounting the feats of Le Loi.

In the twentieth century, one of the keys to the Communist Party's success in Vietnam was its ability to convince ordinary citizens that the party was the keeper of the flame of nationalism. Beginning in the 1920s, leaders of the Vietnamese revolution linked the modern struggle to past sacrifices made to defeat foreign invaders. The party skillfully created national heroes of those who had sacrificed for the revolution. Celebration of this sacrifice gave the party preponderant power to assemble a pantheon of champions with ties to Vietnam's glorious past. Party publications stressed revolutionary continuity and national sacrifice.[21] One experienced reporter told fellow journalist Frances FitzGerald during the Vietnam War that he finally realized the United States and its Saigon ally would never win "when I noticed the street signs in Saigon were named after Vietnamese heroes who fought against foreign invaders."[22]

The idea of a nation was central to Vietnamese revolutionary success, but so, too, was the construction of important symbols of national identity. Throughout the war against the Americans, Ho Chi Minh became one of those symbols. According to historian William Duiker, the communists used Ho's personality to "cement the Party's reputation as the legitimate representative of Vietnamese national tradition as well as the leading force in the Vietnamese revolution."[23] After Ho's death in 1969, he achieved cultlike status in Vietnam and around the world. He came to represent the aspirations of the nation, even if party handlers largely constructed his public persona. The party was so successful in disseminating its message of national unity that political training of citizens beyond the initial indoctrination program was usually not necessary. Ho's national narrative became a dominant fixture in the minds of PAVN regulars marching south.

From the earliest days of the revolution, communist training manuals and political commissars made sure that PAVN and PLAF soldiers understood how the concepts of *dan toc* ("nation," or "the people") and *ai quoc* ("patriotism," or "love of country") merged to form a political ideology that put the cause of national liberation first. The PAVN and PLAF were organically connected to society, its leaders argued, and the communists' support came directly from the people in liberated areas. The connection to the national cause had been underscored throughout the basic training of communist cadres and was constantly reinforced by political officers. At the heart of this training was the notion that the PAVN and PLAF were armies "of the people" that supported national liberation. In every phase of the revolution, therefore, the idea of nationhood was central.

An important—and yet little known—aspect of the Vietnam War is that U.S. allies in South Vietnam also shared this sense of history. No political leader in Saigon denied that the people of Vietnam had a shared past and that cultural and ethnic homogeneity marked Vietnam's national history. Nguyen Cao Ky, South Vietnam's vice premier, wanted to march north against Ho Chi Minh and his followers to unify the country under an anticommunist banner. The political division at the seventeenth parallel between North and South Vietnam was a modern creation with no cultural or historical precedent. Most modern Vietnamese hold at least the perception that the country has a common language, common ancestry, and similar cultural practices. Although there are strong regional differences, the country has enjoyed a sense of unity from its earliest days. Despite U.S. efforts to create a new nation from dust south of the seventeenth parallel, most Vietnamese understood that the political contest in South Vietnam between communist and noncommunist forces was in many ways a battle over who owned the past, and therefore the future, of Vietnam. Any nation-building effort had to begin with the premise that Vietnam was a unified nation with a long tradition of national political movements. That the United States and it allies failed to construct a lasting and victorious state does not detract from the fact that the Vietnamese understood full well the idea of nationhood.

REBUILDING THE IRAQI STATE

Though the Bush administration faces a very different historical and political situation from that faced by Kennedy and Johnson in Vietnam, the goal of building or reconstituting an independent and sovereign state is the same. The first task in nation building in Iraq is bringing its disparate groups together. Taking a page from the Vietnam nation-building experience (perhaps without knowing it), the Bush team argued that creating a strong national army was the place to start. The thinking in Washington was that Iraqis needed to provide for their own security, but in a way that aided the nation-building process. The fear was that without a national army—the National Iraqi Army (NIA)—that was structured along U.S. lines and following U.S. training and operational procedures, each ethnic, religious, and tribal group would maintain its own security force. These forces would then be turned on each other to avenge rivalries that had been subsumed by Saddam's brute use of force. A new national army would also serve the republican experiment in Iraq by providing a blueprint of what society could become: integrated and thinking along national lines. As the Bush administration continues to campaign for the viability of the NIA, the rhetoric is sounding much as it did during Vietnam-era administrations.

After the French decamped from Vietnam, the first action the Americans took there in 1955 was to dismantle completely the Vietnamese National Army, which had had ties to the French colonial government. Nearly half the army inherited from the French was dismissed, and the United States went about creating the Republic of Vietnam Armed Forces (RVNAF) from scratch.[24] Lost in that transfer were years of experience fighting the communists. Still, American military advisers believed that it was better to start with a smaller army composed of U.S.-trained soldiers than it was to use an experienced army that had been trained by France. In Iraq, the Bush administration also discarded experienced soldiers and officers when it created the NIA. Fearing that the army was made up of Baathist supporters of Saddam Hussein, the Bush administration gambled that it could create a new army that had no ties to the old regime. That gamble has had mixed results. Jeffrey Record, a historian writing for the Strategic Studies Institute, has labeled as a tragic mistake the CPA's decision in mid-May 2003 to disband the entire Iraqi regular army with only a month's pay.[25] According to another source:

The dismissal of Iraqi officers treated them as an extension of Saddam and the [Baathist Party's] rule . . . rather than as patriots who had fought for their country. It also added several hundred thousand men to the labor pool when there were virtually no jobs, and it effectively told all officers of the rank of colonel and above that they had no future in a post-Saddam environment. At the same time, it implied to all Iraqis that the National Iraqi Army might be so weak that Iraq would remain little more than a client of the United States and Britain in the face of the threat from Iran and possible future intervention by Turkey.[26]

Indeed, building an army from scratch is difficult enough. Doing it in a time of war is nearly impossible. In both Vietnam and Iraq, U.S. military planners dismissed what could have been the bulk of a new national army, worried that it had ties to the old regime. The United States quickly learned in both instances, however, that those connections probably were not impossible obstacles to overcome.

In Iraq, this problem is particularly acute. According to Stephen Biddle, a senior fellow in defense policy at the Council on Foreign Relations, Iraq's Sunnis now see the NIA as a "Shiite-Kurdish militia on steroids."[27] The problem in a communal conflict, like today's insurgent war in Iraq, is that the national army must represent all sectarian groups or it risks making any national government irrelevant. In Iraq, this means that the army has to mirror the major sectarian groups because the alliance of Shiites and Kurds "would hold real power regardless of what the constitution said."[28] Because Sunnis were cast out of the national army along with Saddam's Baathists, there is the growing feeling among many security experts in Iraq that they will never feel at ease in a coalition arrangement. Most Sunnis are unlikely to support the NIA and, instead, consider it the army of occupation. Finding a way to integrate Sunnis into the NIA remains one of the Bush administration's most pressing problems. If it cannot solve this conundrum, there may be no hope of building a coalition government and avoiding a bloody civil war.

In the summer of 2007, reports from Anbar province highlighted the difficulties facing the Bush administration in helping the Iraqis build a national army capable of uniting Sunnis, Shiites, and Kurds. In a remarkable shift in policy, the U.S. command was now arming Sunni rebel groups that, at one time or another, had fought against the Baghdad government and the National Iraqi Army. American military planners in Iraq turned to this tactic knowing that many Sunni groups had grown disillusioned with al-Qaeda in Iraq. In exchange for American backing and weapons, these Sunni groups have agreed to fight al-Qaeda in Iraq and halt attacks against U.S. troops. Of course, this policy is not without risk. There is no requirement that the newly armed Sunnis in Anbar province will join the national army and certainly no guarantee that these Sunnis will not eventually turn their weapons on government soldiers or American troops. Still, many U.S. officers report that the policy change is a step in the right direction.[29]

In Baghdad, however, the government met this new U.S. approach to bringing Sunnis into the fold with a great deal of skepticism. One of Prime Minister Jawad al-Maliki's closest advisers is reported to have asked why the U.S. command was intent on creating new Sunni militias when the National Iraqi Army's main objective was to destroy Sunni militias.[30] This difference of opinion only highlights the difficulties the Bush administration and the U.S. command have had in moving the Baghdad government and its national army to a policy of reconciliation with the Sunnis necessary to carry out the political part of nation building. In late 2007, some Sunni groups began political assassinations of key provincial and national leaders to derail any U.S. attempt to bring Sunnis in from the cold. It is unlikely that new American weapons or promises of shared oil revenue will stop some Sunnis from striking out at Baghdad and the Shiite community. The process of reconciliation is long and arduous, and steps in that direction have to begin immediately if Iraq is to avoid a bloodier civil war. The prospects for peace do not look good.

TRULY NATIONAL ARMIES

As in Vietnam, another problem facing the Bush administration in Iraq today is getting the newly constituted army ready to assume the bulk of military and security operations. In both wars, U.S. military officials launched an aggressive training program designed to bring the new armies up to speed as quickly as possible. In both cases, that process dragged on far longer than anyone in Washington had anticipated. With each passing month, U.S. military officials in Vietnam and Iraq understood the dangers of having Americans dominate military operations. Still, the new national armies were not ready to take on major responsibilities even after years of training. The dependence on the U.S. armed forces to get the job done in Vietnam and Iraq slowed the nation-building process in both cases and threatened to destroy the credibility of those efforts. In both cases, the NIA and the RVNAF became an "army in waiting." And in both cases, the wait went on far longer than the national armies could afford.

In Vietnam, there were several significant problems with the training the RVNAF forces received. Many of these problems led to poor performance on the battlefield and conflict with civilians. One of the most pressing issues was that tactical instruction programs were hampered by the lack of demonstrations or practical exercises and that training centers never had complete up-to-strength demonstration units commensurate with the large number of trainees.[31] When an operation required five experienced soldiers, the RVNAF troops saw it demonstrated by only two. Throughout the counterinsurgency era, demonstration units were often called away from their posts to put down a village uprising. Obviously, it is difficult to simultaneously fight today's insurgency and train tomorrow's soldiers. This is an age-old problem, one that will likely define the Iraq experience. There never seems to be enough time to train local forces to do the job that needs doing immediately.

Language and culture also provided impediments to successful training programs in Vietnam. American officers instructed in English using U.S. manuals. This was not a problem for most officers, but for enlisted men the language gap proved difficult to overcome. As for Iraq, how many U.S. training experts in Iraq speak Iraqi Arabic, Najdi Arabic, Kurdish, Chaldean, or Assyrian? Even if the training is handed over to Iraqi officers, as many administration officials insist is already happening, at some point in the training process an American must communicate complicated goals and strategies to someone from a completely different culture. As the war dragged on in Vietnam, and strategic doctrine changed, many of the training manuals were not properly updated. Only in 2004 did the U.S. Army issue its new counterinsurgency training guide for soldiers in Iraq, the first since Vietnam. Outdated manuals, poor instruction, and the lack of live demonstrations combined to make the training experience miserable for everyone.

To compensate for insufficient training, U.S. advisers in Vietnam eventually instituted a combined operations program, sending RVNAF troops out with their U.S. counterparts.[32] Despite this program's success, it could not make up for all the deficiencies in RVNAF training. Nor could it create confidence in South Vietnam's armed forces. The trend in Iraq today is likewise toward more combined operations. There have been reports that U.S. troops will also mirror Iraqi police because of the many abuses in regional jails. If this is true, it is an alarming trend. A key element of success in building up national security forces is the crossover point, where the national troops and police can take up the bulk of operations. Despite public rhetoric to the contrary, events on the ground in Iraq suggest the United States is not sufficiently confident in Iraqi security forces to hand over major security and policing responsibilities. Former secretary of defense Melvin Laird has argued that it is essential to reach this crossover point as soon as possible. In an essay in *Foreign Affairs*, Laird suggested that "the administration must adhere to a standard of competence for the Iraqi security forces." When that standard is met, U.S. troops "should be withdrawn in corresponding numbers."[33]

VIETNAMIZATION AND IRAQIZATION

Laird was describing for Iraq the old policy of "Vietnamization" used to give more responsibility to the South Vietnamese armed forces. Laird's boss, Richard Nixon, described the policy this way: "We have adopted a plan which we have worked out in cooperation with the South Vietnamese for the complete withdrawal of all U.S. combat forces and their replacement by South Vietnamese forces on an orderly scheduled timetable. This withdrawal will be made from strength and not from weakness. As South Vietnamese forces become stronger, the rate of American withdrawal can become greater."[34]

U.S. strategy in Iraq is remarkably similar. President Bush hopes one day to turn over a majority of military and security operations to the NIA while withdrawing U.S. ground forces. The White House has been particularly optimistic in its predictions that the NIA can handle the job and that the time for the transfer of responsibility is drawing near. The administration initially promised that the U.S. troop withdrawal would begin by the end of 2007, following the success of the surge. Secretary of Defense Robert Gates has now said he wants time to reevaluate U.S. troop levels and security in Iraq before any more troops can be brought home. At this writing, it looks as if one hundred thousand U.S. troops will still be in Iraq when the new American president is sworn in late in January 2009.

The pause that Gates now says is necessary comes after years of optimistic predictions about U.S. troop withdrawals. After the December 2005 elections in Iraq, General Martin Dempsey, the U.S. commander of the Multinational Security Transition Command, said the crossover point was approaching. In a teleconference from Iraq, Dempsey reported that roughly one hundred battalions of Iraqi army soldiers were conducting security operations throughout the country and that another twenty-seven battalions of special police were providing a "bridge between combat and operations and civil police operations."[35] An Iraqi navy, an Iraqi border patrol, an Iraqi air force, and seventy-five thousand Iraqi police joined these security forces. Despite the general's optimism, the Bush administration is not prepared to turn over major responsibilities to the Iraqis just yet. In an important policy speech in January 2006, President Bush backed down on his earlier promise of withdrawal, suggesting that by the end of the year the goal was to have Iraqi security forces "control more territory than the Coalition."[36] The president also expected that the United States would withdraw two of the seventeen coalition brigades by June 2006, hoping that Iraqi security forces could make up the difference.[37] As events unfolded in Iraq, however, that timetable was pushed back.

The Iraqis are experiencing difficulties in training and may not be ready to assume new responsibilities by the end of 2008. According to retired U.S. general Paul D. Eaton, who was in charge of training the NIA, poor planning, insufficient staffing, and inadequate equipment hampered the effort.[38] The general reported being dumbfounded when administration officials in May 2003, just one week after the president's "mission-accomplished" speech, told him he would be sent to Baghdad to begin rebuilding the NIA. Immediately, Eaton faced staffing problems. Promised 250 professional staff members, he began the training exercises with less than half that number. At no time during Eaton's eighteen months in Iraq did he have the proper staffing. He was also without adequate equipment to train the NIA. According to Eaton, he had to "scrounge" for even the most basic military supplies: "We were told to find anything we needed for the soldiers—boots, canteens, rucksacks, belts, beds, blankets—from Iraqi sources where possible."[39] Walter Slocombe, senior civilian adviser to the administration on national security and defense in Iraq, concurred with Eaton's assessment: "I have to agree with General Eaton, that it was hard to get the resources we needed out there. There was not a broad enough sense of urgency in Washington."[40] Of course, the decision by the Bush administration not to preserve any of Saddam Hussein's army exacerbated problems with training.[41]

Poor training usually leads to poor battlefield performance, and this was certainly the case in Iraq and Vietnam. In Iraq, the NIA's Second Battalion quickly dissolved after its initial contact with insurgents at Fallujah in April 2004. The Iraqi troops were simply not ready for combat or for criticism from locals. Some Fallujah residents called them "collaborators," and this had a devastating impact on troop morale. Although some important adjustments were made following the debacle at Fallujah, significant doubts remain about the viability of the NIA. Many military analysts fear that prematurely giving the NIA responsibility for the war against the insurgents will have damaging effects on Iraq's future. Others fear that the NIA's dependence on U.S. troops is the most debilitating aspect of security operations in Iraq. All agree, however, that in 2008, after one year of the surge, the Iraqi army is still not yet ready to take over military and security operations completely.

In Vietnam, the RVNAF faced the same tough circumstances. During the first few years of the RVNAF's contact with PLAF regular-infantry units, the South Vietnamese experienced significant defeats at Ap Bac, Song Be, and Ba Gia. Shortly after the battle of Ba Gia in 1965, the Intelligence Committee of the U.S. Mission in Saigon cabled Washington indicating that RVNAF losses at Song Be and Ba Gia had been higher than expected[42] The reports also suggested that the psychological toll of these defeats could lead to the "collapse . . . of the will to fight" on the part of the South Vietnamese forces, and that U.S. troops would probably have to be used to avert such a disaster.[43] On June 7, General William Westmoreland sent a long telegram to Washington outlining the difficulties:

In pressing their campaign, the Viet Cong are capable of mounting regimental-size operations in all four ARVN [Army of the Republic of Vietnam] corps areas, and at least battalion-sized attacks in virtually all provinces. . . . ARVN forces on the other hand are already experiencing difficulty in coping with this increased VC capability. Desertion rates are inordinately high. Battle losses have been higher than expected; in fact, four ARVN battalions have been rendered ineffective by VC action in the I and II Corps zones.[44]

Westmoreland saw "no course of action open to us except to reinforce our efforts in SVN with additional U.S. or Third Country forces as rapidly as practicable during the critical weeks ahead."[45]

Consequently, on June 7, 1965, Westmoreland requested an additional forty-four battalions (roughly 150,000 men) for Vietnam and permission to go on the offensive.[46] He believed he could halt communist advances by deploying U.S. troops along the coast and near the major southern cities. He would then send units into the central highlands to block any communist attempt to control Highway 9 (a major east–west road) and sweep to the sea in an effort to divide the country. After securing the coastal areas, the cities, and the highlands, Westmoreland believed he could launch search-and-destroy missions with U.S. forces that would eventually grind down the enemy and diminish its will to continue the fight. The general would also rely on massive U.S. firepower, including the bombing of North Vietnam. Finally, the pacification effort in the countryside would provide enough local security for the government's programs to take hold.

President Johnson eventually agreed with Westmoreland's request. In the spring and summer of 1965, U.S. combat troops were introduced into Vietnam, and their operations shifted from mainly defensive to mainly offensive. With this change in policy and doctrinal thinking came a change in the relationship of the South Vietnamese army to the war and the nation. The official U.S. policy of assuming the responsibility for the major offensive military missions unfortunately relegated the RVNAF to static defensive operations.

From 1965 until 1968, then, the South Vietnamese were passive actors in their own counterrevolution. This doctrinal shift signaled to the RVNAF troops that their major benefactor did not think they could go toe to toe with the PAVN and PLAF. This demoralizing experience had a dramatic impact on the conduct and outcome of the war. After taking over the war completely, the Johnson administration handed the war back to the RVNAF in 1968, hoping to silence protestors in the streets in the United States and rescue the 1968 election for Vice President Hubert Humphrey. Hoping to foster self-help and self-reliance for South Vietnam, Johnson began integrating RVNAF forces into major military operations with their U.S. allies. The process was accelerated in the Nixon years, but by then it was too late for the South Vietnamese to rally themselves. The communists simply had too many military, political, and social advantages for the South Vietnamese to launch a successful counteroffensive.

In retrospect, it was a mistake for the United States to take over the Vietnam War completely. Over time, U.S. forces looked to much of the world like an occupying army, and the RVNAF lost confidence in its own ability to defend the nation. The Bush administration certainly faces the same problem in Iraq. The problem is how to balance security needs with Iraqi needs to provide that security themselves. What is clear, however, is that the Vietnam experience cannot be repeated. The United States needs to hand major security operations over to the Iraqis as soon as possible or the nation-building effort is sure to fail. If the Iraqi security forces cannot come together to form an alliance with common dreams and aspirations around a meaningful political agenda, Iraq will be a failed state.

Authoritarian rule was one of the few reasons for the success of the fragile alliance created by the British at the end of World War I. From 1920 until 1958, the pro-British monarchy held disparate groups together by force and with massive amounts of British aid. There were constant protests and other signs of discontent throughout the pro-British period, but all were put down with brute force. In 1958, King Fayisal II was overthrown by an anti-British, anti-Israel coalition of pan-Arab supporters. One coup after another led to an increasingly unstable Iraq during the 1960s and early 1970s. Through it all, the Iraqi national armed forces tried to maintain political control and stability through the use of force. In 1961, Kurds in northern Iraq began a rebellion that many experts would argue continues to this day. When the Baathists took power in the 1970s, they promised to end the Kurdish rebellion and to put down the Shiite independence movement in southern Iraq. Saddam Hussein took control of the Baath Party and the country in 1979, increasing the Sunni hold on power. Hussein created a strong central state with a civil administration that was extremely loyal to the party. Hussein made little effort to bring Kurds and Shiites into the national government or the armed forces.

The United States is now facing an uphill battle as it tries to bring these disparate groups together through sheer force of will. Without a natural coalition against their enemies, Baghdad faces an uncertain future. Years after the national elections, there is still considerable debate over the face of the government, especially the prime minister's office. Increased sectarian violence only adds to the likelihood that the government will not survive. Iraq may have had all the essential elements of a state in the twentieth century, but there is little evidence of nationhood. The army was never an army of the people; rather, it came to represent one sectarian group at the exclusion of the others. The Sunnis, who once controlled the armed forces, are now the subjects of its raids. The Kurds have an increasing role to play in the national army, but they, too, remain outside the corridors of power. The history of modern Iraq does not inspire confidence in the ability of the state to convince its citizens of a shared national past and a common future.

Despite these serious shortcomings, the Bush administration initially declared Iraq stable enough for some U.S. troops to come home. In a television address to the nation on September 12, 2007, President Bush assured Americans that it was time to get a return on the success brought about by the surge in Iraq. For the first time since the war began in March 2003, the president announced a limited withdrawal of U.S. troops. The plan called for fifty-seven hundred troops to be redeployed from Iraq by the end of 2007 and another eighteen thousand to be withdrawn by July 2008 if all goes well. But Gates and General David H. Petraeus have now suggested that these will be the end of the troop withdrawals as they reassess the security and political situation in Iraq. These modest troop reductions will do little to shore up confidence in Baghdad and may even undermine much that the Bush administration is trying to accomplish. There is also support in Congress for greater troop reductions on a more advanced timetable, regardless of the military condition of the National Iraqi Army. At the other end of the spectrum, some U.S. military leaders wonder if troop withdrawals are really in order. They argue the United States should be increasing—not decreasing—its military presence in Iraq, precisely because the Iraqi armed forces are not handling the problems of security and nation building well.[47]

THE SOCIOECONOMIC VIABILITY OF THE STATE

Compounding the problems in building up effective armed forces in Iraq, as in Vietnam, are crippling political and social issues. In a protracted war, the socioeconomic viability of the state is more decisive than its ability to win or lose battles. Eventually, the government in Baghdad will have to deliver the goods or it risks the same fate that met the Saigon government. During the Vietnam War, Saigon's inability to manage its own affairs ultimately proved just as devastating as communist attacks. The Saigon government routinely spent 50 percent of its budget on non-defense-related items.[48] The United States supported these expenditures directly but never provided enough maintenance to meet rising needs or costs. By 1965 the South Vietnamese deficit had mushroomed to unmanageable proportions, and inflation was approaching unprecedented levels. According to Jeffrey Clarke, the chief historian at the Center for Military History, consumer prices in South Vietnam rose 900 percent between 1964 and 1972; the cost of rice rose an unbelievable 1400 percent.[49] Military personnel on fixed salaries felt these economic strains intensely. During that same period, the salaries of enlisted men rose only 500 percent, despite fifty redress actions.[50] RVNAF troops routinely complained about the lack of food, poor housing, overcrowded barracks, insufficient medical attention, and dismal pay.[51]

The rest of South Vietnamese society also felt these economic and social pressures. With rising inflation rates and a growing dependence on imports, the average citizen lost ground. Because of graft and corruption in the importation program, this once-proud exporter of foodstuffs now imported most items—even rice—at inflated prices. The government could do little to control inflation or the black market, and it lost the confidence of the people of South Vietnam quickly. Without massive amounts of U.S. aid, the South Vietnamese government would not have survived long on its own. The twenty-year nation-building experiment in Vietnam quickly turned into twenty years of extraordinary dependence, subsidies, price supports, economic credits, and kickbacks. Is this what is in store in Iraq? The United States has just built the largest embassy in the world in Baghdad, so perhaps policymakers in Washington are planning on a lengthy dependence.

The Bush administration believes that Iraq is making substantial social progress and that eventually its rich oil reserves will save it from dependence on U.S. aid. These optimistic predictions do little to change the fact that Iraq has suffered enormously from U.S. economic schemes. Limited economic growth has come mainly from foreign companies that have taken over newly privatized industries. Rejecting the high modernization projects of the Vietnam War designed to show Saigon's national energy and state support for civil society projects, the CPA instead privatized much of the nation-building effort in Iraq, leaving the Iraqi economy in a shambles. Iraqi unemployment remains unusually high and the inflation rate is staggering.[52] Foreign investment is improving, but mostly in foreign-owned or -operated entities. A basic question must be asked: Are Iraqis better off now than they were before the U.S. invasion? Scores of reports suggest that the average Iraqi citizen is only slightly better off today than before the invasion, in economic and social terms. In several key areas, the U.S. nation-building effort has actually created more problems than it has solved. For example, the 2005 per capita income in Iraq was $3,400 per year, just ahead of Cuba's. The 2005 unemployment rate was 25 percent, a figure that would have been significantly higher without jobs in the U.S.-supported armed forces.[53] In 2005, only Zimbabwe had a higher annual inflation rate than Iraq's 40 percent.[54]

Bob Herbert of the *New York Times* reported in early 2006 that despite the infusion of $16 billion in American taxpayer money, "virtually every measure of the performance of Iraq's oil, electricity, water, and sewage sectors has fallen below prewar levels."[55] Herbert's sources were U.S. government witnesses who had testified before a U.S. Senate committee hearing.[56] Although there has been some improvement in a few vital social areas since the 2003 invasion, after five years of nation building most Iraqis expect more. A common criticism of the Bush administration is that it simply cannot keep the lights on in Baghdad, fueling distrust and anxiety throughout the country.

Some critics of nation building, however, maintain that the social aspects of political war are overrated. Stephen Biddle has suggested that security is still the most important problem facing the Bush administration in Iraq. In his view, "Survival trumps prosperity."[57] In an essay in *Foreign Affairs*, Biddle asked, "Would Sunnis really get over their fear of Shiite domination if only the sewers were fixed and the electricity kept working?"[58] This is an important question, one the Bush administration continues to wrestle with. If the Vietnam War is any guide, and I think it is, the president would be wise to develop social programs that integrated Sunnis, Kurds, and Shiites into a unified economy and a national government if at all possible. All U.S. aid should be dependent on Baghdad's willingness to create a government of reconciliation and concord. So far, it has failed miserably in this regard.

At the end of U.S. involvement in Vietnam, Saigon was losing control of the population at an alarming rate. Failed social and political programs in South Vietnam quite possibly would have toppled President Thieu even without PAVN military advances. Proper sanitation and dependable electricity are important elements in any nation-building program. They are clear signs that the government is viable. Security is essential for these programs to take root, but ignoring the political war to concentrate only on security is a tragic mistake. It does matter who is collecting the garbage on Tuesday and whether the lights work. The building of a civil society is dependent on sound thinking and active programs. No number of publicity stops in once-violent areas of Baghdad can replace sound economic and social plans. Only after Iraqis take ownership of civil society programs will the government in Baghdad have the full support of its citizens. This is the war's most pressing problem because so little progress has been made on this front.

In retrospect, the Bush administration made a huge error in ignoring the U.S. intelligence community's warnings about the perils of nation building in Iraq and in scrapping the recommendations of the Future of Iraq Project. The narrow focus on spreading democracy through military strength has led to several pitfalls. Today's U.S. armed forces are perhaps the best in modern history, but even they cannot alone carry the nation-building effort. As in Vietnam, what is needed in Iraq is a combination of security and social programs. In Vietnam, the United States took over the shooting war completely and left the political war to the South Vietnamese. The Saigon government failed miserably in addressing basic social and economic problems, and as a result, it lost the confidence of its own people. The communists were formidable adversaries; but the lack of social progress in South Vietnam doomed the nation-building experiment there. Even among those who understood the need to mix security with social programs, security came first. According to most policymakers in Washington, the United States had to provide enough security in South Vietnam for the social programs to take hold. It now seems clear, however, that security and social progress must proceed in tandem, or nation building cannot succeed.

After five years, finally there are signs that the Bush administration and military planners in Iraq are starting to understand the social needs of ordinary citizens. In early 2006, Major General Richard Zilmer and Lieutenant General Peter Chiarelli started to emphasize the political war against the insurgents. For General Zilmer, U.S. commander of the dangerous Anbar province, getting to know the needs of Iraqis has been one of the most important tasks. Along with providing security, the general also made sure that local health care workers and police officers were being paid enough to keep them on the job. He knew the ten largest employers in the province

and worked closely with them to make sure they continued to operate effectively. For General Chiarelli, reconstruction of the basic infrastructure went hand in hand with providing security. Both
generals hoped that promoting economic growth and development
in the most impoverished areas of Iraq would dissuade Sunnis from
joining the insurgency.[59] And of course, General Petraeus has been
an outspoken advocate of attention to the political side of the war
since the American invasion began in March 2003. Still, some in
Washington wonder aloud if this emphasis on the political war and
social issues has come too late.[60]

MODERNIZATION AS IDEOLOGY

In both Vietnam and Iraq, the social aspects of nation building rested
on a strong belief in modernization theory among key policymakers
in Washington. During the cold war, many U.S. officials believed that
newly emerging postcolonial nations could be brought into an alliance with the United States against the communists through economic and political development. Social scientists working on
problems of development in the 1950s, such as economist Walt Rostow, argued that modernization was a phased process that would
bring poor nations from subsistence to abundance and would promote freedom through a series of developmental stages common to
all states.[61] At the most advanced stages were the United States and
much of Western Europe. Less developed countries, especially peas-
ant societies in Latin America, Asia, and Africa, needed to follow the
U.S. model, Rostow claimed, to advance to their fullest potential.[62]

Modernization was evolutionary, not revolutionary, the argument went, and it promised to free "backward" societies from the meddling of the communists from Moscow and Beijing. With careful political oversight and massive economic development aid, the United States could guide these newly emerging nations through the international minefield. At the core of Rostow's thesis was the belief that societies in the developing world would have to drop their traditional, ethnic-based practices and instead adopt Western structures and thinking. Lyndon Johnson's plan for a Mekong Delta project along the lines of the Tennessee Valley Authority, to help Vietnam end the bonds of misery born out of material want, was classic modernist thinking. He never fully understood that the purpose of the communist revolution in Vietnam was to replace with a different one the very social structure Johnson wanted to impose there. The president favored a liberal capitalist blueprint for society, one the Marxists surely rejected. Modernization in the forms of direct foreign investment and a market economy would eventually come to Vietnam, but only after twenty years of contested cultural negotiations in Hanoi.

In Iraq today, the Bush administration faces many of the same modernization problems that plagued Kennedy and Johnson. Should Iraq develop its post-Saddam political and economic infrastructure along Western lines? Despite enormous efforts to ensure that the government and the economy will fit the local cultural and social climate, many critics of the U.S. nation-building effort in Iraq think the Bush administration learned nothing from the U.S. experience in Vietnam, especially in the area of economic development. This experience proved that billions of U.S. dollars in economic development aid is not enough to mend the problems of failed states. South Vietnam had very little to show for all the "modernization" that took place there. At the end of the day, economic development did little to stop the communists or to convince many South Vietnamese citizens to support the government in Saigon. If Iraq is to have a different fate, the United States must pay attention to the pressing social issues brought forward by the Iraqis themselves. After five years of war, however, it may be too late.

THE STATE AND THE INDIVIDUAL

If average Iraqi citizens are to embrace nation building, the government has to provide a meaningful outlet for political yearnings and protect civil and human rights. In Vietnam, the lack of tangible democratic elections and a poor record on constitutional issues led the citizens to view the government with suspicion. During the war, the government decided not to expand suffrage, and Saigon leaders did all they could to eliminate the political opposition.[63] Despite U.S. efforts to the contrary, Saigon's officials believed that their own personal power was more important than the nation-building experiment. Although never happy with the outcome, no U.S. administration protested the fixed elections in 1955, 1967, or 1971 or the antidemocratic nature of the government. The elections were little more than fig leaves to mask a seriously flawed political structure and successive administrations that failed to capture the support of the people.

Perhaps most damaging to the people of South Vietnam was the feeling that the political process was run by a small group of people connected to a secret party with its own security force. Throughout the war, the Can Lao Party, much like a nineteenth-century American political machine, controlled much of the politics in Saigon, and the structure made it impossible for people to rise in politics or do business in South Vietnam unless they belonged to the Can Lao. The party had no recruitment drives or membership applications. Instead, party officials chose potential members. Once in power, the Can Lao ruled absolutely. From 1959 until the end of the war in 1975, citizens were routinely arrested without formal charges and held indefinitely. Can Lao officials often censored the press, and when editors refused to cooperate, their papers were shut down. Attacks against Buddhists by the largely Catholic Can Lao became legendary, but those attacks also extended to labor leaders and students. In short, any critic of the Can Lao–dominated government became an enemy of the state.

The lack of protected rights and the government's inability to deliver social goods eventually led the people of South Vietnam to turn their backs on the Saigon regime. Many subsequent revisionists of the war tend to blame Congress or the press for the U.S. defeat in Vietnam. It is important to remember, however, that long before Congress pulled the plug on funding the Vietnam War, the South Vietnamese lacked confidence in their government. In the war's last months, President Nguyen van Thieu's government actually received a vote of no confidence from the National Assembly because of its inability to provide basic goods and services and his government's crackdown on civil liberties.[64] Rice wars erupted during the last two years of the war, since many South Vietnamese citizens lacked enough food to eat. Once an exporter of basic foodstuffs,

South Vietnam had grown so dependent on U.S. imports and subsidies that it became an importer of key meal ingredients, even rice.[65] Throughout the war, ordinary citizens took to the streets in Hue, Da Nang, and Saigon to protest the government's lack of civil reform. The U.S. nation-building effort was doomed not only because of poor decision making in Washington but also because the Saigon government failed to meet the needs of its people.

If Iraq is to have a different fate, the government in Baghdad will need to ensure its citizens' social progress and protect basic civil and human rights. Since the U.S. invasion of Iraq, there have been three elections, and a new constitution has been established. There have been problems with each, and the trick now is for the United States to disengage and give the Iraqis a chance to attack these problems for themselves. The biggest political obstacle for the government in Baghdad is how to increase participation and bring voices of opposition into the process. Reports from Iraq in January 2006 suggested that the security police are less than impartial. Since Shiites dominate the police force, they can easily exact revenge on their Sunni neighbors. Many Sunnis complain regularly about police brutality and about torture at the hands of the national police.[66] The Iraqi Islamic Party, the largest Sunni political group, claims that the national police routinely round up its members. In some areas south of Baghdad, Sunni homes have been confiscated by the national police and redistributed to Shiite friends and families.[67] Some Sunnis fear that the Shiite-dominated government in Baghdad will not reach out to its Kurdish and Sunni neighbors.

Perhaps the most trying issue facing the Bush administration is that its nation-building experiment in Iraq demands patience from the American public. The process of building strong civil and military institutions is arduous and time-consuming, often with so few tangible results in the first years that the public can grow tired of waiting for success. The difficulty for Bush—as it was for Kennedy, Johnson, and Nixon—is that he has already spent considerable goodwill disproportionate to the results. Once the gap between intentions and accomplishments widens, as it has in Iraq, the public loses faith in what the administration has to say. After it was revealed that there were no weapons of mass destruction in Iraq, the public started to drift. When Bush officials claimed in early 2005 that the suicide bombers were the last gasp of the insurgency, the public started to question the efficacy of the war.[68] Then the administration declared that the surge would produce dramatic results and that the Iraqi government would reach the congressional benchmarks. In every public opinion poll, the president and his Iraq policy fail to capture public support.

If nation building is to be successful in Iraq in this crucial year, the Bush administration would be wise to look carefully at events in Vietnam. During the Vietnam War the United States did a poor job monitoring social and economic progress. Is it time to focus less on the noble goal of spreading democracy in the Middle East and more on social and economic progress in Iraq? Are the two dependent upon each other, as the Bush administration believes? Some experts believe the Bush administration can back off its quest for total democracy in Iraq and save the government in Baghdad by emphasizing social progress and constitutional rights. In their view, the best export America can send to Iraq is not necessarily democracy, but support for human and civil rights and social and economic progress.

Journalist Fareed Zakaria has criticized the Bush administration's insistence on transplanting democracy to Iraq as missing the point. In his view, Washington should accept a "liberal autocracy" in places like Iraq because this type of government can get the job of nation building done without the distractions of democratic politics.[69] Even the American version of democracy did not flourish overnight, he contends, and liberal autocracies might be able to deliver the social and economic programs needed to stabilize the nation-building effort.

At the crux of this argument is the belief that constitutional protections of basic human and civil rights, combined with social and economic justice, may be more important than holding elections and having majority rule. Critics of the Bush administration point to the remarkable progress made in places like Taiwan, Singapore, Indonesia, and Thailand as proof that the Iraqis may be willing to forgo democracy for a few decades in exchange for constitutional protections and economic progress.[70] It is an interesting argument, and one that will no doubt continue even after the dust has settled in Iraq. There is no doubt, however, that Zakaria is right about the need for something less than total democracy in Iraq. Alongside constitutional protections and social justice, greater focus on per capita income is essential. The data are clear that democracies cannot thrive when the annual per capita income falls below three thousand dollars.[71] Unfortunately, the average Iraqi still hovers near this failure mark despite enormous oil revenues for the state and private firms.

Many Bush administration officials, however, doubt that it is possible to have constitutional protections and economic progress without democracy. As part of the preparations for elections in Iraq, the Bush administration asked a group of U.S. and Iraqi experts on democracy and constitutional rights to oversee the development of a series of laws to provide the blueprint for democracy and justice in Iraq. These experts operated under what became known as the Transitional Administrative Law (TAL). On March 8, 2004, they submitted their recommendations.

The TAL called for the establishment of several democratic institutions in Iraq to support the nation-building effort there. It created a presidency council, a prime minister's office, and a congress with a system of checks and balances in place to ensure that no single entity would have too much power. The presidency council held a veto power, but that veto could be overridden by the congress. The TAL also established an independent court system that protected basic civil liberties. No citizen could be held without charge, and every Iraqi had the right to a fair and speedy trial. The rights of all minority groups were preserved and protected by law and the independent judiciary. In short, the TAL promised many of the constitutional guarantees secured in the U.S. Constitution. In practice, however, these constitutional protections are often overlooked.

Furthermore, is mirroring the American political and constitutional system the best thing for Iraq? In Vietnam, there were three national elections, two constitutions, a National Assembly, and an independent judiciary. At no time, however, did a majority of the people of South Vietnam believe that the government was viable. Despite an enormous nation-building effort by the United States over twenty years, Washington could never guarantee that these democratic institutions would live up to their responsibilities. Security issues overwhelmed all else. It was impossible to insist that Saigon move on much-needed social reforms, because the war was going so badly in the countryside. In leaving the political war up to Saigon, the United States failed to ensure that pressing social and political issues would be properly addressed.

In Iraq, the Bush administration's insistence that democracy be the cornerstone of any nation-building effort has meant that many social concerns have also been left for another day. Significant progress has been made on a number of fronts, but severe hardships still lie ahead. At some point, the Bush administration must permit the NIA to stand on its own, and the Iraqi security police will need to put aside ethnic and religious differences. All Iraqis must believe in a common future together if there is to be any hope of success. Social progress can help advance this process and is essential in any nation-building effort. The United States has already stayed on too long in Baghdad, and the Iraqis have met the same fate as the South Vietnamese: social unrest, dependence, and resentment. Moreover, the American public has lost all patience with nation building and the long war in Iraq. Americans expect progress from the blood and treasure they expend. That is another lesson the Bush administration should have learned from Vietnam.

CHAPTER FOUR

STAYING THE COURSE

A S THE Bush administration enters its final year, public support for the war has evaporated. The 2006 midterm elections were a clear mandate for change in Iraq, yet the Bush administration insists that staying the course is the only solution. Still, the president must be troubled by events in the Middle East and the growing public unrest. Blood speaks with a terrible voice, and Bush is no doubt experiencing the same agony that Lyndon Johnson called "his special burden."[1] Three times since 1945 Americans have been sent into harm's way when casualties were in the thousands—Korea, Vietnam, and Iraq—and each time public support for the war declined as deaths mounted.[2] Despite its mandate, Congress has been unable to limit the president's hand in Iraq and now seems content to wait until the 2008 U.S. presidential election is over to pass any binding resolutions on troop withdrawals or spending limits. Although the war occasionally disappears from the front pages of the nation's newspapers, the presidential contest between John McCain and the

Democratic nominee will revise its importance. Senator McCain supports the war effort and is prepared to stay in Iraq for one hundred years if necessary. Conversely, both Senator Barack Obama and Senator Hillary Rodham Clinton promise an immediate drawdown of troops. One of the Democrats' goals is to tie the failing U.S. economy to the war in Iraq, something that is not at all difficult to do.

The problems the Bush administration and Senator McCain face in Iraq are similar to the problems Lyndon Johnson faced in Vietnam. In both cases, according to John Mueller, an expert on war and public opinion, the public gave substantial support to the effort as troops were sent in, but that support evaporated as the war dragged on.[3] Public opinion polls clearly showed that a majority of Americans supported Johnson's 1965 decisions to send combat troops to Vietnam and to give them offensive missions.[4] Likewise, the Bush administration initially enjoyed enormous support from a majority of the American public when U.S. troops invaded Iraq.[5] In each case, however, public support declined sharply in the early stages of the conflict because reluctant supporters were quickly alienated.[6] Although the erosion slowed as approval was reduced to hard-core supporters of the war, overall public opinion never recovered to preinvasion levels. By 1967 less than half the American people supported the war in Vietnam, and that remained the high-water mark for the remaining seven years of the war.[7] For Mueller, Iraq is noteworthy because the decline in public support has been faster than most experts predicted. In his view, this phenomenon has occurred because the American public "places far less value on the stakes in Iraq" than it did on those in Korea and Vietnam.[8]

According to Mueller, most Americans believe that the perceived threats in Iraq—weapons of mass destruction and support for international terrorism—have been discounted. Francis Fukuyama, of Johns Hopkins University's Paul Nitze School of International Affairs, agrees, adding that with those justifications gone, the war in Iraq has become a request to spend "several hundred billion dollars and thousands of American lives in order to bring democracy to . . . Iraq."[10] Most Americans simply do not share the Bush administration's enthusiasm for planting the seeds of democracy in the Middle East. Mueller concludes that the remaining public support for the war probably comes from those who still believe that there is a connection between events in Iraq and international terrorism.[11] As the government in Baghdad continues its struggle to bring Sunnis into the fold and secure a just peace, even this support will decline. The failure of the Baghdad government to meet most of the congressional benchmarks in 2007 was the final nail in the coffin of public opinion.

However, the Bush administration did learn some lessons from Vietnam. Since the invasion of Iraq began, officials have worked tirelessly to keep body bags and flag-draped American coffins from public view. This effort and the absence of a draft probably have kept thousands of young people from marching in the streets, but public support has still disappeared. The press has not been as hostile to Bush as Kennedy, Johnson, and Nixon claimed it was to them, and Congress has done little to rein in the administration in Iraq. During Vietnam, Congress made several attempts to limit the president's ability to wage war, and the U.S. Senate Foreign Relations Committee held important hearings that brought various critics of the administration's actions to testify before the nation, including George F. Kennan, the father of the original containment policy. By the war's end, Congress had passed the War Powers Act, which severely limited the president's actions in war. Specifically, the legislation required the president to inform Congress within forty-eight hours of the deployment of American troops abroad and to withdraw them within sixty days unless Congress approved an extension. President Bush has had unfettered power compared with Vietnam-era presidents.

PROMOTING THE WAR

President Bush does sound like Lyndon Johnson when he is on the stump trying to rally support for the war. Bush often places Iraq in the context of past American struggles for freedom and independence. He uses soaring rhetoric to describe the U.S. commitment to Iraq and has stated frequently that Iraq is the next phase of the American freedom struggle. One of Johnson's favorite tactics was to sell the war to the American public with appeals to their ideals. For example, he often claimed that the principle at stake in Vietnam was the same as that "for which our ancestors fought in the valleys of Pennsylvania."[12] Vietnam, the president declared, was not a war about territory; it was a war to usher in a new era of Asian economic and political development to end "the bondage of material misery" in that part of the world.[13] Johnson was also fond of asserting that most countries would shrink from the burden of responsibility that the United States faced in Vietnam. He lauded America as the "strongest and greatest democracy on earth" and said that only the United States had "the intelligence, the resources, and the will to endure a distant struggle for freedom's sake."[14] Johnson usually ended his policy speeches with some version of this refrain: "We will not be defeated. We will not grow tired. We will not withdraw, either openly or under the cloak of a meaningless agreement. We must stay in Southeast Asia—as we did in Europe—in the words of the Bible: 'Hitherto shalt thou come, but no further.'"[15] Substitute *Iraq* for *Southeast Asia,* and the two Texans sound very much alike.

The problem with appealing to ideals, however, is that such appeals eventually need to be grounded in national security interests, or the nation withdraws its support for the war. During Vietnam, it became more difficult to convince ordinary Americans that all the fighting and dying were worth it. Although most Americans supported intervention in Vietnam in 1965 to stop the spread of communism, by 1967 they no longer believed that goal was of primary importance to U.S. national security. In the absence of an overarching idealistic framework for the war, public support melted away. Saving South Vietnam did not carry the same cachet as saving the world from communism, and too few Americans believed that Vietnam was worth the sacrifice. Johnson's appeal to ideals, much like Bush's today, ran its course, and Americans eventually concluded that the troops should be brought home.

THE CREDIBILITY GAP

The public also lost confidence in the Johnson administration's ability to close the gap between intentions and accomplishments. At the height of the war, when most Americans realized things were not going well in Vietnam, Johnson launched a public relations campaign designed to convince them otherwise. General Westmoreland, who returned to the United States in November 1967 to shore up support for the war, appropriately fired the first volley. Upon arriving in Washington, Westmoreland told reporters, "I am very, very encouraged. . . . We are making real progress." In an important speech before the National Press Club, the general was even more optimistic. He concluded that the enemy was badly hurt and that the war had "reached an important point where the end begins to come into view."[16] He hinted that substantial troop withdrawals would be possible within two years.

While Westmoreland made the rounds in Washington, Johnson organized several committees to go out and promote the war's progress.[17] The president formed the Committee for Peace with Freedom and the Vietnam Information Group to monitor public support and tackle problems as soon as they surfaced. These groups reported that the major obstacle facing the president was the public's misperception that the war was a stalemate. Accordingly, Johnson ordered both groups and the U.S. embassy in Saigon to "search urgently for occasions to present sound evidence of progress in Vietnam."[18] The publicity machine went into high gear, promoting stories about PAVN/PLAF body counts and significant military victories in the Mekong Delta, the heart of the insurgency. For a brief period at the end of 1967, it appeared that the public relations offensive had worked. Polls showed that support for the war, though below 50 percent, was holding steady.[19] The mood in the White House became optimistic for the first time in years.

The events of January 30, 1968, shattered Johnson's hope of fixing the public opinion problem. Early that morning, combined PAVN and PLAF forces attacked 6 major cities, 36 of the 44 provincial capitals, 64 district capitals, and 50 hamlets in what became known as the Tet Offensive.[20] Although the communist forces suffered huge military losses and did not achieve the general uprising many party strategists had hoped for, the offensive was a key turning point in the American public's support for the war. Live television accounts of the battles in key cities, such as Hue and Saigon, convinced American viewers that Johnson and Westmoreland had been deceiving them. Overnight, support for the war fell by nearly 20 percent.[21] Even the venerable television anchor Walter Cronkite, an initial supporter of the war, wondered aloud if the Johnson administration had been misleading the American people. "What the hell is going on?" Cronkite asked. "I thought we were winning the war!"[22]

THE MYTH OF A LIBERAL PRESS

For many Americans, however, Tet and its treatment pointed to what was wrong with the press and its reporting, and not what was wrong with the war. Revisionist histories today incorrectly argue that the "liberal media" purposely distorted events during the Tet Offensive to promote an antiwar message.[23] Some believe that the same could happen in Iraq. Morton Krondracke, a Washington columnist, argued early in the Iraq War that the media could indeed snatch defeat from the jaws of victory in Iraq if they were not constrained. He used the Tet Offensive and the war in Vietnam as his parallels.

Krondracke believed that Tet had been a military defeat for the communists but the media had spun it a different way: "The U.S. media reported the episode as a U.S. defeat, helping convince the American establishment that the war was unwinnable." In his view, a real danger was "that Iraq could become like Vietnam—a self-inflicted defeat."[24] Although the Communist Party did not achieve some of its stated goals during Tet, the Western press had little to do with the outcome of the war. Hanoi's ability to determine the scope and place of battles and to win peasants to its side had very little to do with press reports. The party did take advantage of the Kennedy and Johnson administrations' mishandling of the relationship between the NLF and Hanoi, but this mishandling, too, was not the major cause of the American withdrawal from Vietnam.

The Abu Ghraib prison scandal is a favorite topic for those who think the press is going too far and being too negative in its reporting of events in Iraq. Most critics of the media feel they fixate on negative stories and do not understand the harm they are doing to the American cause. Several press opponents have argued that reporters, especially U.S. reporters, should get on the team.[25]

For those old enough to remember Vietnam, this assessment may sound eerily familiar. On January 2, 1963, RVNAF forces from the army's Seventh Division attacked the PLAF's 261st Main Force Battalion at the tiny hamlets of Bac and Tan Thoi, sixty kilometers southwest of Saigon. Though outnumbered and outgunned, the PLAF stood its ground, shooting down five U.S. helicopters and retreating under cover of darkness without suffering high causalities. The South Vietnamese, in embarrassing contrast, refused to advance under fire and lost sixty men.[26]

In ensuing days, readers of English-language wire services and newspapers were given their first solid indication that the Military Assistance Command-Vietnam (MACV) reports on Vietnam had been overly optimistic and that something had gone terribly wrong. Reporting for United Press International, Neil Sheehan first heard about the debacle in the early afternoon of January 2, 1963. That evening, he and Nick Turner of Reuters took a motorcycle to Tan Hiep, a command post in the northern Mekong Delta. There, in the darkness, John Paul Vann, the U.S. adviser attached to the RVNAF who had fought at Ap Bac, described the battle scene. He told the reporters that a number of mistakes had been made and that the PLAF "were brave men" who gave a "good account of themselves today."[27] The next day, David Halberstam, writing for the *New York Times,* joined Sheehan and Turner at the Tan Hiep command post. The young reporter asked Vann, "What the hell happened?" Vann replied candidly, "A miserable damn performance, just like always."[28] Sheehan and Halberstam filed their reports—and changed the nature of the relationship between the press and the high military command in Vietnam forever.

Sheehan's account was the most detailed, suggesting that Ap Bac had been a "major defeat" and symptomatic of larger problems in Vietnam.[29] On January 7, the *Washington Post* ran Sheehan's story on the front page: "Angry United States military advisers charged today that Vietnamese infantrymen refused direct orders to advance during Wednesday's battle at Ap Bac and that an American Army captain was killed while out front pleading for them to attack."[30] For five consecutive days, Halberstam's stories appeared on page one or two of the *New York Times.* The headlines told the story: "Vietcong

Downs Five U.S. Copters, Hits Nine Others";[31] "Vietnamese Reds Win Major Clash";[32] and "Vietnam Defeat Shocks U.S. Aides."[33] Sheehan's and Halberstam's reports contradicted the most optimistic predictions from the Kennedy White House and suggested that the public was not "getting the facts on Viet-nam, even at this time when American casualties are mounting."[34]

A few days after the negative press reports, Admiral Harry Felt, commander in chief of the U.S. Pacific Command (CINCPAC), flew from Hawaii to Saigon for an inspection tour. When he met with reporters his first night there, he said he did not believe "what he had been reading in the papers." Instead, he insisted that Ap Bac "was a Vietnamese victory—not a defeat, as the papers say."[35] Felt called Ap Bac a victory, he later reported, because the NLF had abandoned the area to the ARVN's Seventh Division.[36] General Paul Harkins, head of MACV, supported Felt's assertions, claiming that the ARVN had "taken the objective."[37] Savvy journalists questioned the logic of these statements: Most knew that this was not a war about territory. Halberstam, recounting the surreal experience some months later, wrote, "We were all stunned at these new rules for guerrilla warfare—evidently the objective now was terrain, not the enemy."[38] Malcolm Browne of the Associated Press was so infuriated by Felt's comments that he challenged the military leader's understanding of guerrilla war. Felt's angry response was "Why don't you get on the team?"[39]

Every Vietnam-era president complained that the media were against him and were reporting events unfairly. Lyndon Johnson believed that the press was the pulse of the American people, commenting once that if he had lost the support of journalist Walter

Lippmann, "he had lost America."[40] Lippmann, a one-time supporter of the president, turned against Johnson and the war in early 1966. In one particularly harsh column, Lippmann wrote that the president had "never defined our national purpose except in the vaguest, most ambiguous generalities about aggression and freedom."[41] Many Americans agreed, and Johnson's approval rating reflected that agreement. From the introduction of U.S. ground troops in March 1965 until the day he left the White House in January 1969, Johnson's public opinion polls and the support for the war dropped steadily.[42]

Not everyone agreed with public opinion polls on the Vietnam War. President Richard Nixon believed there was a "great silent majority" of Americans who still supported the war and would back his policies. In his mind, the vast majority of Americans did not support the antiwar protestors and instead understood the stakes in Vietnam. In a November 1969 speech, Nixon tried to isolate his critics and regain popular support for the war by charging that the antiwar movement was "irrational" and "irresponsible."[43] He called on the "great silent majority" to support Vietnam in its hour of need, and he aimed his dramatic conclusion at the protestors: "North Vietnam cannot humiliate the United States. Only Americans can do that."[44]

President Bush has made a similar charge, suggesting that those in Congress who speak out against the war and the faulty intelligence that led to it are "unpatriotic."[45] During Vietnam the administration also lashed out at Congress, and many members of the Nixon White House claimed that the antiwar protestors were aiding and abetting the enemy. The White House went after its enemies, compiling a list of names to be targeted for investigation and secretly placing wiretaps on many civilians.

Bush has also lashed out at members of Congress for making the Vietnam analogy, saying it "sends the wrong message to the enemy," even though the president himself has used the Vietnam–Iraq comparison on several occasions.[46]

GROWING RESISTANCE TO THE WAR

In the face of opposition from the White House, some members of Congress have also openly likened Iraq to Vietnam, hoping to make waging war in Iraq impossible. In April 2004, during a period of particularly heavy American and Iraqi casualties, U.S. Senator Edward Kennedy (D-Massachusetts) declared in a Washington speech, "Iraq is George Bush's Vietnam."[47] During a subsequent television interview, Kennedy said, "We're facing a quagmire in Iraq, just as we faced in Vietnam." He particularly cited the lack of information: "We didn't understand what we were getting ourselves into in Vietnam. We didn't understand what we were doing in Iraq. We had misrepresentations about what we were able to do militarily in Vietnam. I think we are finding that out in Iraq as well."[48] Kennedy's comments helped convince others to speak out. Former Congressman Harold Ford Jr. (D-Tennessee) also saw similarities between Iraq and Vietnam, concluding, "The gnawing and growing feeling that the goal of achieving U.S.-style democracy in Iraq is unattainable is reminiscent of the feeling that gripped America during Vietnam."[49] His colleague, Robert Byrd (D-West Virginia), rose on the Senate floor to say, "Now, after a year of continued strife in Iraq, comes word that the commander of forces in the region is seeking options to increase the number of U.S. troops on the ground if necessary. Surely I am not the only one who hears echoes of Vietnam."[50]

Indeed, he was not. Several national publications jumped on the Vietnam bandwagon, including *Newsweek,* which ran "The Vietnam Factor" on its April 19 cover. Bob Herbert of the *New York Times* claimed that the United States was repeating the Vietnam experience in Iraq. "We have been there, done that, and now we are doing it again," he wrote in an editorial in September 2004.[51] His colleague at the *Washington Post,* Robert Kuttner, editorialized that the Iraq conflict "is becoming more and more reminiscent of the Vietnam disaster. American troops mostly stay in heavily fortified barracks. When they do venture out, their sweeps don't achieve durable pacification. Militants and young men of fighting age are long gone by the time American bombardments start."[52] Lawrence Freedman, professor of war studies at King's College in London and one of the most respected military historians in the world, wrote, "Just as Vietnam became McNamara's war, Iraq has become Rumsfeld's war."[53]

In November 2005, House member John Murtha (D-Pennsylvania) stunned his colleagues by calling for the immediate withdrawal of U.S. troops from Iraq. Murtha, one of the top House Democrats on military spending, said U.S. troops were the primary target of the insurgency and that Americans had become a "catalyst for violence."[54] In a speech reminiscent of the intense Vietnam-era debates in Congress, Murtha concluded it was time to bring the troops home.[55] The usually hawkish Murtha set off a firestorm in Washington that concluded with a Senate vote to press the Bush administration for concrete steps toward troop withdrawals but drew sharp protest from Vice President Richard Cheney. Cheney told reporters that politicians who compared Iraq to Vietnam and criticized President Bush were engaging in "dishonest and reprehensible" behavior.[56] Murtha fired back about "guys who got five deferments and [have] never been there and send people to war, and then don't like to hear suggestions about what needs to be done."[57] Cheney had not served in the military, whereas Murtha is a highly decorated Vietnam veteran.

Another Vietnam veteran, William Nash, a retired U.S. Army major general who also served in the Persian Gulf and Bosnia, and who now is a senior fellow at the Council on Foreign Relations, argues that Iraq and Vietnam are eerily similar. In his view, the United States is once again fighting a protracted war with the wrong tactics. "Now we have Vietnam. You've got a sovereign government over there, a big embassy, and 140,000 U.S. soldiers. And our ability to influence political decisions is finite."[58] Similar comments have come from Anthony Zinni, a fellow Vietnam veteran who also served with U.S. forces in Somalia and who preceded Tommy Franks and John Abizaid as chief of the Central Command in the Middle East. Zinni has noted a similarity between Iraq and Vietnam because of the flaws in overall military strategy in both cases. "Some strategic mistakes are very similar," and in both cases the White House was trying to "draw the American people into support of the war by cooking the books. We did it with the Gulf of Tonkin situation . . . and here we have had the case for WMD as an imminent threat for not using international authority to go in."[59]

Even supporters of the war in Iraq are drawn to the Vietnam analogy. Presidential hopeful Senator John McCain has repeatedly used the debacle in Vietnam as evidence that the United States needs to stay in Iraq for the long term. McCain was also an early advocate of sending more U.S. troops to Iraq, over the loud objections of the Bush White House. Early in the war, Secretary of Defense Donald

Rumsfeld often claimed that 132,000 U.S. troops could defeat the insurgency in Iraq. An angry McCain publicly disagreed, stating, "The simple truth is that we do not have sufficient forces in Iraq to meet our military objectives." McCain concluded his remarks with a prophetic warning that if the United States did not send more troops, it would risk "the most serious American defeat on the global stage since Vietnam."[60] Several other Republicans joined McCain in calling for more troops, arguing that in their absence the United States would face "another Vietnam."[61] Most supporters of the war in Iraq believe it was lack of troops, lack of political will, and lack of public courage that led to the American withdrawal in Vietnam. They do not want to see a similar pattern emerge in Iraq, and therefore, they use Vietnam as the backdrop of all their comments on policy decisions. Supporters and critics, then, use the Vietnam analogy to make their case about the war in Iraq.

CONGRESSIONAL CRITICS

During the first two years of the war in Iraq, President Bush encountered few in his own party who opposed the conflict on general principle. Only Chuck Hagel (R-Nebraska), a Vietnam veteran, openly criticized the administration on the war. Hagel's protest, though unusual in the early stages of the military campaign in Iraq, picked up steam during the 2006 midterm elections. Several Republican members of the House broke with the president over the war, and by the summer of 2007, a handful of important Republican Senators— Richard Lugar (R-Indiana), Pete Domenici (R-New Mexico), Lamar Alexander (R-Tennessee), and Judd Greg (R-New Hampshire)—had joined Hagel in calling for a phased withdrawal from Iraq. Still, Republicans in Congress have kept Democrats from passing a timetable for withdrawal or other restrictive legislation. The votes on Iraq fall predominantly along party lines. According to some public opinion experts, the partisan divide over the war in Iraq is considerably greater than it has been for any U.S. military action over the past half century.[62] Furthermore, as political scientist Gary Jacobson noted, President Bush's overall approval rating is also more partisan than that of any president, including Bill Clinton, Ronald Reagan, Jimmy Carter, and Richard Nixon, over the same period.[63] The president, therefore, has won all the support he can expect to get from his fellow Republicans in Congress and across the nation, and even that support is dwindling. Democrats see the war in Iraq as one of the major election issues in 2008 if they can tie it to the failing U.S. economy. The partisan divide, however, is not likely to change how the public feels about the conduct of the war in Iraq. Whatever support the Bush administration had in early 2006 following the national elections in Iraq is probably the high-water mark it can enjoy for the remainder of the war, no matter how successful the military surge has been in Baghdad and Anbar province.

Lyndon Johnson did not even receive partisan support for his policies in Vietnam. During Johnson's five years in office, his most strident opponents were often members of his own party, and usually former Senate colleagues. Richard Russell (D-Georgia), Mike Mansfield (D-Montana), and J. William Fulbright (D-Arkansas) became outspoken critics of Johnson's war. Fulbright charged that under Johnson's presidency, the United States had fallen victim to the "arrogance of power." He argued that Washington was showing "signs of that fatal presumption, that over-extension of power and mission, which brought ruin to ancient Athens, to Napoleonic France and to Nazi Germany."[64] Other liberals in Congress questioned the significance of Vietnam, asking if it was indeed vital to U.S. national security interests. Furthermore, they argued that the high cost of the war was diverting attention from more urgent social problems at home, hoping to revive Johnson's attention to his own Great Society program.[65] Some in Congress challenged Secretary of State Dean Rusk's view that the United States needed to stay the course in Vietnam to convince its allies that it honored its commitments.[66] Indeed, these dissenters suggested that the British, French, and Germans opposed the war and wanted the United States to announce a withdrawal.

Johnson had conservative critics as well. Several conservative members of Congress charged that the president was not "fighting the war to win."[67] They believed that the war in Vietnam was crucial to the larger cold-war struggle. If the United States did not succeed in Vietnam, they feared, the communists would take failure as a signal that America was weak and that other newly emerging postcolonial nations were up for grabs. These hawks viewed antiwar demonstrators with suspicion, and some believed the press had a liberal bias.[68] Most argued that Johnson was preventing the military from doing what it did best—fighting and winning wars. Many said Secretary of Defense Robert McNamara and his civilians at the Pentagon were wrong to limit the war, and some in Congress openly challenged the president to attack North Vietnam directly, no matter the consequences.[69] Representative Mendal Rivers, a conservative Democrat from South Carolina, told the president to "win or get out," summing up the feeling of many in Congress.[70]

Johnson focused much of his attention on his conservative critics, an emphasis that might have cost him his presidency. When public opinion and much of Congress turned against the war in early 1967, Johnson still tried to appease his conservative challengers. He rejected Westmoreland's 1967 request for an additional two hundred thousand troops, and he rebuffed McNamara's proposal to limit or stop the bombing. To placate the conservatives and his own Joint Chiefs, Johnson significantly expanded the list of bombing targets and, for the first time, authorized strikes against bridges, railways, and military barracks near Hanoi, Haiphong, and the Chinese border. By trying to stand firm on the middle ground, however, Johnson wound up alienating his base of support, liberals and southern Democrats. In retrospect, Johnson might have been well advised to pay more attention to the antiwar protestors and his own party. When public opinion turned solidly against the war and his presidency following the January 1968 Tet Offensive, he had little choice but to step aside and let another Democrat represent the party in the November presidential elections.

Richard Nixon also had difficulty keeping Congress and public opinion behind his Vietnam programs. Like Johnson's, many of Nixon's critics came from his own party. One of Nixon's most outspoken opponents was Republican Jacob Javits, a Republican senator from New York. Javits criticized Nixon for doing little to end the war.[71] He insisted the president pay serious attention to public opinion polls that suggested most Americans supported an immediate withdrawal from Vietnam. After the Nixon administration invaded Cambodia in the spring 1970, several Republicans in the Senate cosponsored resolutions that, if passed, would have severely limited the president's power in Vietnam. In June 1970 the Senate voted overwhelmingly to terminate the 1964 Gulf of Tonkin Resolution, which had granted Lyndon Johnson unusual presidential power to wage war. Senators John Sherman Cooper (R-Kentucky) and Frank Church (D-Idaho) cosponsored an amendment to cut off all funds for U.S. military operations in Cambodia by June 1970. Mark Hatfield, a Republican from Oregon, cosponsored a bill with the liberal George McGovern (D-South Dakota) that would have required the Nixon administration to withdraw all U.S. forces from Vietnam by the end of 1971. Although none of these restrictive measures passed either house of Congress, it was clear by 1970 that Congress no longer supported the war in Vietnam.

Eventually, Nixon's enemies in Congress far outnumbered his friends. Even before the 1972 Watergate scandal, the president faced growing opposition to his Vietnam policies. On two separate occasions, the Senate approved binding resolutions that would have required the president to remove all U.S. troops from Vietnam by a specific date if Hanoi cooperated on the release of U.S. prisoners of war. In both cases, the House removed the deadline and watered down the resolution. Still, Nixon knew his hands were tied. Even though he and his National Security Adviser, Henry Kissinger, assured the South Vietnamese leadership in Saigon that the White House would see the war through to the bitter end, both men knew clearly by 1971 they had little support for extending the war much further. It was only a matter of time before Congress, acting on the wishes of the American people, would cut funding for the war or demand a complete U.S. withdrawal.

Will the same be true of Iraq? Will Congress cut funding or demand a timetable for withdrawal? So far, the new Democratic majority in Congress has been unable to muster the votes needed to challenge the president's policies. In July 2007, Senate Democrats put forward a resolution that would have required the Bush administration to begin a phased withdrawal of U.S. troops within 120 days. The vote for the measure was fifty-two yeas to forty-seven nays, but that was not enough to meet Senate rules that required sixty yea votes on this resolution. Senate Majority Leader Harry Reid (D-Nevada) wanted desperately to tie funding of the war to a withdrawal measure, but he simply lacked enough support from both sides of the aisle.[72] The final two 2008 Democratic presidential candidates, Hillary Rodham Clinton and Barack Obama, supported Reid's measure.

In October 2007, the House passed a resolution to give the Bush administration two months to present a withdrawal plan to Congress. This resolution had overwhelming bipartisan support, probably because it required so little of the White House. The resolution did not require the withdrawal of U.S. troops, only an administration report on planning for redeployment. In addition, the White House is required to report to Congress every ninety days on the overall military program in Iraq. This bill does not go far beyond the initial authorization bill in 2003. The lack of teeth in the House version of this measure angered many antiwar Democrats, and it is unlikely that the House leadership will get much in the way of binding legislation.

If congressional Democrats have not been able to force the president's hand through binding legislation, they have continued to apply public pressure on the administration. In September 2007, in a scene eerily reminiscent of congressional hearings on Vietnam, General David H. Petraeus testified before Congress on the progress of the military surge and the continued nation-building efforts in Iraq.

He suggested that American troops and their Iraqi counterparts had significantly increased security in key areas of Baghdad and Anbar province and had "dealt numerous blows to al-Qaeda in Iraq."[73] He concluded, "Coalition and Iraqi security forces have made progress toward achieving security. As a result, the United States will be in a position to reduce its forces in Iraq in the months ahead."[74]

Several members of Congress were openly critical of the general's optimistic report. House member Tom Lantos (D-California) argued that the GAO report released in August 2007 measuring Baghdad's performance on congressional mandates did not support General Petraeus's testimony. According to the GAO report, "Key legislation has not been passed [in Iraq], violence remains high, and it is unclear whether the Iraqi government will spend $10 billion in reconstruction funds as promised."[75] Lantos also pointed to a highly skeptical report issued by retired Marine Corps general James L. Jones, who had been charged by Congress with investigating progress in Iraq. "No amount of charts of statistics will improve its [the administration's Iraq policy] credibility," Lantos declared in the hearings.[76] In the Senate, Hillary Rodham Clinton also made reference to the GAO report, highlighting the fact that Baghdad had failed to meet fifteen of the eighteen congressionally mandated benchmarks for continued support.

The performance of the Iraqi government is where Democrats in Congress and presidential hopefuls Barack Obama and Hillary Clinton will no doubt focus their criticisms during the 2008 elections and beyond. By tying the failures of the al-Maliki government to the $1 trillion price tag for the war in Iraq, Democrats will try to make the link between the high cost of the war and the U.S. economic meltdown. Historically, Americans have voted with their pocketbooks in times of economic strife. Only time will tell if the Democrats' message resonates with American voters. What is clear, however, is that Republican supporters of the war, including presidential nominee John McCain, will be saddled with questions about the Bush administration's credibility on the war.

THE CREDIBILITY FACTOR

During the Vietnam War, the fear of what might happen in South Vietnam and to American credibility if the United States withdrew kept the United States bogged down. President Johnson complained repeatedly that he could not "get in deeper" and that he could not "get out."[77] At the heart of that conundrum was the realization that withdrawal carried with it some painful consequences. The Bush administration has accepted Colin Powell's formulation of the problem in Iraq. Borrowing from the Pottery Barn (though he denies the attribution), Powell said: You broke it, you bought it. In other words, many key people on the Bush team thought that withdrawing from Iraq before the job is done borders on the criminal because the United States introduced instability with its invasion. In sum, Washington must see the process through until an independent Iraq can stand on its own. A certain circular logic to this justification is indeed reminiscent of the Vietnam War.

Lyndon Johnson frequently insisted that the United States could not simply withdraw from Vietnam because U.S. credibility was on the line.[78] American prestige was at stake in the jungles of Vietnam, Johnson reasoned, and he was not going to let down his allies. Johnson feared that other nations around the world would no longer trust the United States if it withdrew from Vietnam. How ironic, then, that it was Johnson's European allies, nations whose trust and confidence carried such weight among U.S. administration officials, who turned against the war and U.S. policy in Vietnam. From early 1962, leaders in NATO-allied France, Germany, and Britain, America's most important NATO and European allies, argued for a neutralist settlement to the crisis in Vietnam and a U.S. withdrawal.[79]

Johnson neither heeded their advice nor, in fact, even heard what they were saying. Instead of withdrawal, Johnson tried to convince his European allies to join him in the fight in Vietnam. He called his coalition of the willing the "many flags approach."[80] The problem for Johnson, however, was that not one European ally agreed with the U.S. position in Vietnam. An angry Johnson once begged British prime minister Harold Wilson to send at least one "British cook to Vietnam" so that the United States could claim that its allies supported its Vietnam policy.[81] When Wilson refused, Johnson bellowed, "Maybe you never got your copy" of the SEATO treaty, requiring Britain and the United States to defend South Vietnam.[82] Wilson's response was to publicly criticize U.S. bombing raids over North Vietnam and suggest that the United States seek a negotiated settlement.

Of course, Johnson was also concerned about personal credibility. Much of what drove him was the desire not to be the first president to lose a war.[83] He was especially fearful of the difficulties that President Harry S. Truman and the Democratic Party had faced over charges in 1949 that the president had "lost China." Following Mao's victory in China, the U.S. Congress had erupted in accusations that Truman had been "soft on communism" and "asleep at the wheel."[84] Johnson would not let a debate over Vietnam wreak similar damage on his administration. Such a debate, Johnson concluded, "would shatter my presidency, kill my administration, and damage our democracy."[85] Above all, Johnson feared that the conservative members of his own party, especially powerful southerners in key congressional leadership positions, would "push Vietnam up my ass every time" if he did not intervene and South Vietnam was eventually lost.[86] Obsessed with not appearing weak, Johnson often repeated he was not going to be the first president to "turn tail" and run or "be shoved out of a place."[87] No, Johnson concluded, "we've got to conduct ourselves like men."[88]

This mixture of international and personal credibility fueled much of the fire over Vietnam: The United States had to intervene in Vietnam to show its allies it lived up to its treaty commitments. Once it was engaged, there was no easy exit. Senator George Aiken (R-Vermont) once suggested that the United States simply declare victory in Vietnam and go home. Considerable support existed in Congress for withdrawal, but there were also members who believed that Johnson had to get "in deeper" to win. The Joint Chiefs continually pressed the president to widen the war by mining Haiphong harbor and increasing the bombing around Hanoi and the Ho Chi Minh Trail. Johnson rejected these suggestions, but he clearly felt pressure from both sides to settle the Vietnam issue once and for all.

By 1967, several of Johnson's key supporters and advisers no longer believed that the "psychological domino theory" should keep the United States in Vietnam. The first dissenter was Robert S. McNamara. As early as 1965, the defense secretary had had doubts about the efficacy of the military campaign in Vietnam. He feared that the United States could not accomplish its political goals

through the application of military force. Although McNamara supported the war in public, in private he was skeptical that the United
States would prevail. By summer 1967, McNamara and Undersecre-
tary of State Nicholas Katzenbach were convinced the United States
could not win in Vietnam at acceptable costs and should seek a negotiated settlement.[89] Much of their thinking was influenced by
National Intelligence Estimates and Central Intelligence Agency reports, such as the JASON study, which suggested that U.S. bombing
raids had failed to diminish Hanoi's will to fight.[90] Appearing in August 1967 before a special Senate subcommittee investigating the air
war, McNamara testified that the bombings were not having the desired result. He warned the senators that "the air war in the North
was no substitute for the ground war in the South, that bombing
would not allow us to win on the cheap."[91]

In early November 1967, McNamara further distanced himself
from the war by sending Johnson a memorandum that argued for an
American withdrawal.[92] McNamara urged the president to rethink
the U.S. commitment to Vietnam: "Continuation of our present
course in Southeast Asia would be dangerous, costly in lives, and un-
satisfactory to the American people."[93] Unbeknownst to McNamara
at the time, Johnson had ordered CIA director Richard Helms to in-
vestigate what would happen to U.S. credibility abroad if the United
States withdrew from Vietnam. In a September 1967 report, seen
only by the president and his national security adviser, Walt Rostow,
Helms and his CIA analysts reported that "if the United States ac-
cepts failure in Vietnam, it will pay some price in the form of new
risks which success there would preclude." But, they also concluded
that "the risks are probably more limited and controllable than most

previous argument has indicated."[94] Johnson ignored Helms's report and fired McNamara, and the war raged on for another eight years. In the end, it would appear that Helms and McNamara were correct.

Despite his strong misgivings about the war, as well as his very public stance against its escalation in 1967, McNamara came to symbolize all that was wrong in Vietnam. In the Kennedy years, many congressional critics found McNamara arrogant, too sure of himself and his policies. After 1965, when the conflict in Vietnam escalated into an American war, McNamara was the Johnson administration's key architect and policy spokesperson. He constantly briefed Congress and the American public on the significant progress being made in the war, and he warned detractors they would be on the losing side of history. He delivered this message with a sureness that made many in Washington nervous. His personal style turned many supporters against the war, and his insistence the administration was on the right track in Vietnam only underscored the growing congressional doubts about success there. When the military began to have misgivings about the limited-war strategy in Vietnam, McNamara became the focus of their ire. He was an easy, even if undeserving, target for their frustrations.

Forty years later, Secretary of Defense Donald Rumsfeld likewise found himself overidentified with the war in Iraq and its failures. Once again, military leaders questioned the leadership capabilities of the secretary of defense. Rumsfeld's insistence that the United States was on the right track in Iraq, despite growing evidence to the contrary, prompted many former military leaders, including generals with leadership experience in Iraq, to call for his resignation. From his first days at the Pentagon, many of Rumsfeld's detractors pointed to a similarity in personality and style between Mc-Namara and Rumsfeld. Nixon's secretary of defense, Melvin Laird, described Rumsfeld as having an "overconfident and self-assured style on every issue," a style that turned many in Congress and the military against the administration.[95]

Several members of Congress feared that the Bush administration was repeating many of the Johnson administration's mistakes and that Rumsfeld was indeed doing his best to impersonate McNamara. At the core of the problem, in their view, was the idea that U.S. credibility was again at stake.[96] As in Vietnam, critics of the war in Iraq suggested that the administration, especially Rumsfeld, was not being realistic about the consequences of a U.S. withdrawal. After Rumsfeld's resignation in November 2006, those criticisms were leveled directly at the president. Only one major European ally has joined the "coalition of the willing"—Great Britain—and others, such as Spain and Italy, have withdrawn their troops altogether. The Bush administration counters that there has not been another attack on American soil since the invasion of Iraq, and that troops will not be withdrawn completely until the job is done. Furthermore, supporters of the war in Iraq believe a U.S. withdrawal before the coalition government can stand on its own will tell the terrorists that their goal of creating more theocratic states can be achieved simply through the shedding of American blood.

Consequences of Withdrawal

In Iraq, talk of a U.S. withdrawal stokes fears of a subsequent bloodbath. The Bush administration rightfully worries that premature withdrawal from Iraq will precipitate more chaos and a bloodier civil war there. The president seems determined to stay the course in Iraq to prevent such a fate, even if it means extending the U.S. commitment beyond the public's willingness to support such a measure. Many observers in Washington see no easy way out.

On the one hand, if the Bush administration stays too long in Iraq, American citizens will grow weary and press their representatives to alter U.S. foreign policy fundamentally, as occurred following the Vietnam War. An "Iraq syndrome" will join the "Vietnam syndrome" in dominating all foreign policy discussions. If, on the other hand, the Bush administration pulls out of Iraq before the government can stand on its own against the insurgents, that same public will no doubt compare Bush's policy to that of Nixon's "decent interval."

Throughout 1971 and 1972, Nixon and his National Security Adviser, Henry Kissinger, made it clear to Hanoi and its allies in Moscow and Beijing that the United States was willing to strike a deal to end the war following the November 1972 U.S. presidential elections. Kissinger secretly met with Chinese premier Zhou En-lai in Beijing on July 9, 1971, in preparation for Nixon's 1972 visit. Kissinger told Zhou the United States would exchange its complete withdrawal of U.S. troops for the return of American prisoners of war and a cease-fire throughout all of Indochina. Kissinger declared that Nixon would need a guarantee that there would be an interval— described variously as "a reasonable interval," "a sufficient interval," and a "decent interval"—between the cease-fire and a resumption of hostilities between North and South Vietnam.[97] In a follow-up meeting, Kissinger pressed his Chinese host on the timing of such hostilities, arguing they could not resume immediately. "All we ask,"

Kissinger concluded, "is a degree of time so as to leave Vietnam for Americans in a better perspective."[98] If a month after an American withdrawal "the war starts again, it is quite possible we would say this was just a trick to get us out and we cannot accept this. If the North Vietnamese, on the other hand, engage in a serious negotiation with the South Vietnamese, and if after a longer period it starts again after we are all disengaged. . . it is much less likely that we will go back [to Vietnam] again."[99]

The skillful Zhou pressed Kissinger to clarify his meaning. The Chinese wanted an end to the Vietnam War, too, and were perfectly willing to trade on Hanoi's wishes for better relations with the United States. Zhou wanted to see how far Kissinger was willing to go toward peace and asked, "So the outcome of your logic is that the war will continue?" Kissinger replied, "Why should we be afraid of socialism in Vietnam when we can live with communism in China?"[100] That was all Zhou needed to hear. The Nixon administration was pursuing a dual track in Vietnam. The first track was to continue to apply military pressure on Hanoi through the mining of Haiphong harbor, increased bombing raids against North Vietnam, and U.S. military incursions into Laos and Cambodia designed to break up communist supply routes and sanctuaries. The second track, and the more likely scenario, was the "decent interval." The United States would withdraw its troops completely in exchange for American prisoners of war and a guarantee that a reasonable amount of time would pass between the U.S. pullout and the resumption of hostilities. But how long was enough?

Nixon believed that the timing of the decent interval was crucial to his foreign policy goals. He supported Kissinger's stance in China and, in fact, had endorsed it in several White House meetings with his national security adviser. He pressed Kissinger, however, on the long-term consequences. Nixon wondered if the anticipated North Vietnamese defeat of South Vietnam would cost his administration too much and if Kissinger could guarantee a decent interval. The president asked how the United States could gain control of events in Vietnam without troops on the ground.[101] Kissinger answered, "If a year or two years from now North Vietnam gobbles up South Vietnam, we can have a viable foreign policy if it looks as if it's the result of South Vietnamese incompetence."[102]

The president liked the plan, as long as it would coalesce after the 1972 U.S. presidential election. When South Vietnamese president Nguyen van Thieu realized what Kissinger and Nixon had in mind, he wept openly. The Nixon administration would eventually ask South Vietnam to sign an agreement that forced a U.S. withdrawal, released U.S. prisoners of war, and provided no military or political guarantee for the security and longevity of South Vietnam. South Vietnam was being forced to commit suicide. However, Nixon and Kissinger had done their homework. They recognized that there was little support in the United States for prolonging the war after the election that the Saigon government had called for in 1971. More important, the Saigon government had lost the faith of a majority of the American people.

In that election, President Thieu won by a landslide, primarily by disqualifying his political opponents. The Nixon administration had previously pressed the Thieu government to hold new elections from early 1969 on. A reluctant Thieu eventually agreed to the proposal, and elections were scheduled for October 1971. Thieu had narrowly won favor in 1967, and he feared that any new election would carry with it the potential of ousting his government. The economy was in a shambles, the communists had made huge advances since the beginning of the phased American withdrawal, and public support for the war inside South Vietnam was diminishing rapidly. Furthermore, Thieu understood that the American public was growing tired of supporting the war in Vietnam. Still, Thieu could not bear the possibility that he might lose an open election. Accordingly, he did everything in his power—which was considerable—to ensure that no serious challenge would be made to his rule.

The Nixon administration was outraged by Thieu's behavior. During negotiations in Paris, the Communist Party's chief diplomat, Le Duc Tho, suggested to Kissinger that the United States could withdraw from Vietnam under the cover of elections if Washington worked hard to guarantee that all qualified candidates were in the pool.[103] According to Tho, Thieu would lose any national election that included candidates who would be willing to negotiate a ceasefire and settlement with the National Liberation Front.[104] Therefore, Tho reasoned, the United States could claim that Thieu had been deposed legally, and Hanoi would have a legitimate shot at regime change in Saigon. From the time the Paris negotiations had been made public, it was Hanoi's official policy to insist that the United States stop offering its unconditional support to Thieu. The communists believed that they could take South Vietnam through the moral superiority of their political program if only they were allowed a reasonable chance in national elections. The Nixon administration had rejected this call during its first two years, but by 1971 there was some support for an open election in Saigon.

Despite the Nixon administration's efforts to force Thieu into a truly democratic election, the South Vietnamese president managed to keep the election a one-man race. Early in 1971, Thieu learned that South Vietnam's vice president, Nguyen Cao Ky, was interested in running for the nation's highest office. Thieu used a technicality in a newly approved election law to disqualify Ky. General Duong van Minh (known in the West as Big Minh) also wanted to run. Minh was on record as approving open negotiations with some NLF leaders, although he had stopped short of endorsing a fully negotiated settlement. After Thieu had eliminated Ky's candidacy, the U.S. embassy in Saigon supported General Minh's presidential aspirations. Apparently, U.S. ambassador Ellsworth Bunker had tried to bribe Minh to run in order to make the election look "more democratic."[105] In the end, Thieu was the only candidate for the office of President of South Vietnam. He used funds from the CIA to win reelection by a landslide by buying votes. The Nixon administration learned that it could not count on democratic elections in South Vietnam to bring peace or to precipitate an American withdrawal.

Today, in Iraq, there are similar fears. The congressional benchmarks for progress in Iraq—established with the military surge—have not been met, and there is a growing belief in the United States that all parties in Iraq are simply waiting for a U.S. withdrawal to begin a full-scale civil war. Senator Carl Levin (D-Michigan), chair of the Senate's Armed Services Committee, believes there is little hope of avoiding a civil war in Iraq because of "the desperate situation that their people find themselves in, and recent discussions among top Iraqi political leaders have apparently produced little or nothing. That failure had reinforced the widely held view that the current

Iraqi government, led by Prime Minister Maliki, is nonfunctional and cannot produce a political settlement because it is too beholden to religious and sectarian leaders (like Mr. [Moqtada al-]Sadr)."[106]

Furthermore, many U.S. policymakers have been openly critical of the Bush administration for not changing the geometry in Iraq the way Nixon and Kissinger did in Vietnam, despite the sorrowful and tragic ending to that war. Most realists today question the wisdom of staying the course in Iraq when it appears the Bush administration has lost control of the war and its meaning. Some have even suggested the president was presented a golden opportunity to revise U.S. thinking on Iraq and to construct a U.S. withdrawal from the recommendations of the Iraq Study Group. The long-anticipated Iraq Study Group report, issued in December 2006 by study group chairs Lee Hamilton and James Baker, provided the president with some strategic thinking and a carefully thought-out exit strategy. According to the report, the United States must launch "a new diplomatic offensive to build an international consensus for stability in Iraq and the region. This diplomatic effort should include every country that has an interest in avoiding a chaotic Iraq, including all of Iraq's neighbors." The report also tied Baghdad's political and social performance to continued U.S. aid and recommended a reorganization of American troops in the region.[107]

Of these recommendations, the most important was the call for regional negotiations. Sensing that few states in the region wanted to see the conflict in Iraq spill over its borders, the authors of the report called on Washington policymakers to take the lead in creating a framework for regional negotiations that would isolate the terrorists operating in the region from the growing civil war in Iraq. Iraq's six contiguous neighbors—Kuwait, Syria, Jordan, Saudi Arabia, Turkey, and Iran—would become shareholders in the problem and the solution in Iraq much the way China and the Soviet Union had in Vietnam. Some appropriately applied incentives and punishments would complete the deal while the United States reorganized its military presence in the region. The Iraq Study Group correctly understood that the United States did not need to withdraw from the Middle East altogether; in fact, few would benefit from that development. Instead, a reorganization of the U.S. presence and mission would reposition the United States as an honest broker in dealing with the complex problems of the Middle East rather than perpetuate the perception in the minds of some in the region that the United States is the power that hurts Islam. A deescalation of the violence inside Iraq, coupled with regional negotiations, held the best promise for long-term peace and stability, the report concluded.

Most pundits and policymakers were shocked when the Bush administration rejected the Iraq Study Group's recommendations and instead launched the military surge in January 2007. Perhaps the surge was some masterful strategic plan to escalate the violence to buy time for a more advantageous moment to implement the Iraq Study Group's recommendations? That has not been the case. Instead, the Bush administration has increased the U.S. military presence inside Iraq without making any significant advance in the political or diplomatic realms. The problem is, of course, that the war has taken on a regional significance that makes it impossible to put the genie back in the bottle. The Bush administration's policies in Iraq have ensured that terrorist groups throughout the region would come to Iraq to push their larger agendas. This was not the case in March

2003, when the United States invaded Iraq. There is little evidence that international terrorists operated within Iraq's borders with Saddam Hussein's permission. Instead, the chaos created by the war in Iraq has pulled terrorists to that country. In fact, most intelligence reports make clear that al-Qaeda in Iraq formed only in 2005, two full years after the United States invaded the country.

The Bush administration's rejection of the Iraq Study Group's recommendations on regional negotiations is mind-boggling. If the Bush White House does not embrace regional diplomacy and begin to build a framework for negotiations to end the war, the situation in Iraq will no doubt get worse before it gets better. There is simply no solution to the complicated problems in Iraq that does not involve statecraft.

THE HIGH COST OF WAR

Staying the course in Iraq has had a disastrous impact on American power and prestige in the region, and sadly, it will take years for the United States to rebuild its position. Furthermore, the war—now America's second longest foreign war—has created huge problems at home. Despite looming deficits, a failing economy, and unexpected expenses attributed to Hurricane Katrina and other natural disasters, policymakers in Washington have spent an average of $6.8 billion per month in Iraq since the March 2003 invasion. Many Americans think this money would be better spent in other ways, and the next president will find it impossible to ask Congress for additional funds for the war if Baghdad doesn't meet the congressional benchmarks. Eventually, the next president may face the same conundrum that haunted Lyndon Johnson: how to pay for an unpopular war in a time of economic troubles.

For Johnson, the answer came in the form of a war surtax. Convinced he needed to continue to fund his Great Society social programs and also the war in Vietnam, Johnson reluctantly introduced a special personal income tax in January 1968. Within three months, he expanded that tax to include business profits. Johnson announced the 10 percent surtax shortly before the Tet Offensive, making the American public all the more skeptical of his plans. Johnson had rejected such measures throughout the first three years of his presidency, but by late 1967, it was clear that he had no choice but to raise taxes to pay for the war's growing costs.

Old cold warriors Dean Acheson, Paul Nitze, and W. Averell Harriman believed the United States faced a serious financial crisis if it could not control the war's costs. For these three giants of the cold war, that crisis had the potential to be far more damaging to U.S. security interests than the loss of South Vietnam to Ho Chi Minh. They urged Johnson to rethink U.S. policy in Vietnam, and to get a handle on costs. Adding to Johnson's troubles was a major meltdown in the British economy, causing a significant drop in value of the British pound sterling. The fallout was that U.S. gold slipped in value, losing over $370 million in trading during a single day.[108] According to Dean Acheson, Harry Truman's secretary of state, the gold crisis dampened "expansionist ideas" in Washington, forcing the president to reject Westmoreland's new troop-increase request in early 1968.[109]

Financial crisis and declining public support for the war following the January 1968 Tet Offensive forced Johnson from office. On March 31, 1968, the president announced he would not seek nor would he accept his party's nomination for the 1968 presidential election. A dejected Johnson spent his remaining months in office desperately seeking an end to the war in Vietnam and full funding for his Great Society programs. He got neither. Instead, Johnson presided over the origins of the first modern, sustained U.S. economic recession, which would last from 1968 until the early 1980s. This economic downturn represented the first time since World War II that the American economy did not rebound. The economic growth so characteristic of the early cold-war years had given way to massive deficits, trade imbalances, and new regressive taxes. In the end, Lyndon Johnson found it impossible to maintain public support for both his war and his social programs. He could not have guns and butter.

THE WAR AT HOME

The Bush White House has been fortunate that the American public is registering its disapproval of the war only through public opinion polls and the voting booth. President Bush has been spared the massive antiwar protests that Johnson and Nixon experienced. During the Vietnam War, hundreds of thousands of protestors took to the streets. Perhaps the most significant protests were the massive national moratoriums against the war held in Washington, D.C. In October 1967, antiwar protestors gathered in Washington for seven days of speeches, songs, and marches. The most dramatic protest came on October 21, 1967, with a march against the Pentagon. As many as thirty-five thousand protestors walked from the Lincoln Memorial across the Potomac River to the "nerve center of the war."[110] They formed a human chain around the Pentagon, trying to levitate it and exorcise its evil spirits. Many protestors tried to convince soldiers protecting the building to leave their posts. Toward the end of the evening, a serious clash broke out between antiwar activists and federal marshals who had been called in to keep the peace.

Two years later, protestors staged another march on Washington in November, which brought nearly 1 million people to the nation's capital. The protest was part of a larger strike against the war organized by the National Mobilization Committee to End the War in Vietnam (MOBE). In mid-October, MOBE had organized demonstrations in over fifty American cities. Crowds of over one hundred thousand had gathered in Boston, San Francisco, Philadelphia, and New York. With this success, MOBE joined forces with other antiwar groups to launch the national moratorium for November. Unlike the first march on Washington, however, the 1969 national moratorium featured middle-class Americans and gold-star mothers opposed to the war. They read the names of the American dead and placed placards bearing these names in coffins positioned outside the gates of the White House. Many mothers carried the names of the sons they had lost in the war. In many ways, the protest movement had matured. This dramatic shift had a profound impact on public opinion. Throughout the early years of protest, many Americans found the radical elements of the antiwar movement more unsettling than the war itself. By 1969, however, the antiwar movement had gained momentum in middle-class homes and communities.

Returning Vietnam veterans also began to speak out against the war, making it more difficult for Richard Nixon to continue to escalate the conflict. In one dramatic protest in April 1971, now known as Dewey Canyon III, Vietnam veterans returned their medals to Congress after making angry speeches about the war. During that protest, a young John Kerry appeared before the Senate Foreign Relations Committee, asking, "How do you ask a man to be the last man to die for a mistake?" Kerry was a member of a group called Vietnam Veterans against the War (VVAW), an organization that had considerable influence in some middle-class communities.

Although growing numbers of Iraq War veterans are organizing against the war, their numbers are small compared with the membership of the VVAW. Cindy Sheehan's 2004 protest at the Bush ranch over her son's death and the war in Iraq does not yet mirror a larger trend. The Bush administration has been spared the volatility of the 1960s and 1970s, but it does seem clear that the American public has had enough. The most telling sign of Iraq's place in the American landscape is that no Republican candidate for national office is likely to run as a "Bush Republican" in 2008. Instead, most Republicans are trying to distance themselves from Bush and the war in Iraq. Even Senator McCain has been careful to draw sharp distinctions between his policies and the president's as he runs for the nation's highest office. Iraq and President Bush will be the two most unpopular issues of the 2008 election. Whoever wins the White House will be forced to change course in Iraq.

CHAPTER FIVE

CHALLENGES TO AMERICA'S POWER

IN DUSTING off John Foster Dulles's liberation rhetoric of the 1950s, neoconservatives in the Bush administration challenged the world's tyrants, threatening to roll back advances made by evil across the globe under more compromising U.S. administrations. The major difference between the Eisenhower years and 2003, however, was the undying belief of Bush officials in the efficacy of conventional military power to achieve its objectives. Few administrations have embraced the notion that the world could be remade by American military power as securely as the Bush team. They argued that "history could be pushed along with the right application of power and will."[1] But history teaches a different lesson. The American experience in Vietnam proved that U.S. military power was not omnipotent, that the United States could not solve complicated political problems with force alone, and that there were indeed limits to what the United States could do by sheer will. Despite overwhelming force, technological superiority, and abundant financial resources, the United States was fundamentally incapable of coping with the enormous political complexities that inevitably emerge from a protracted military conflict. The United States never lost a significant military engagement in Vietnam, but neither could it use that enormous power to end the war on acceptable political terms.

In rejecting the lessons of Vietnam by pursuing a war of choice in Iraq, the Bush administration has endangered U.S. foreign policy for years to come. No president wants to be saddled with limitations, especially in the realm of foreign affairs. But the recklessness of the Bush administration, with its undying Wilsonian views about democracy promotion, has handcuffed our next president. There will be an Iraq syndrome—an unwillingness to engage the outside world for fear of another Iraq—that places severe limits on what the president can do in foreign affairs. Already many in Congress have sworn off U.S. involvement in global crises, and in some cases, such as Darfur and Kenya, the United States needs to be a major party to the solution. Such limitations reveal the weaknesses of a global power when its power is used unwisely. By going to war in Iraq, the Bush administration mortgaged America's standing in the world and its ability to influence world events.

The Bush administration's insistence on using America's preeminent power for democracy promotion in the Middle East was part of a larger strategy to maintain U.S. predominance in the post-cold-war era. The grand irony of the Bush team's revolutionary agenda has been that America's old cold-war rivals, China and Russia, have actually increased their projectible economic and military power while the United States has been bogged down in Baghdad. Furthermore, the poor U.S. economy, partially caused by the long war in

Iraq, has allowed friends and foes to increase their economic leverage globally. The dollar has dropped significantly against many foreign currencies, and the outlook for the U.S. economy is bleak. All of this suggests that the United States has actually lost power and prestige in the world while fighting a war to increase U.S. power and prestige in the Middle East. After five years of war in Iraq, Americans are re-learning what they had already learned in the mangrove swamps and central highlands of Vietnam so many years ago.

In Vietnam the United States learned that there were indeed limits to American power. The policies of the "can-doers" Lyndon Johnson surrounded himself with could not do much to alter events in Vietnam. The United States spent over $167 billion in Vietnam but had very little to show for it. "The high hopes and wishful idealism with which the American nation had been born had not been destroyed" in Vietnam, a reporter for *Newsweek* observed, "but they had been chastened by the failure of America to work its will in Indochina."[2] Indeed, defeat in Vietnam caused a great crisis of will among those Americans who had once believed in the boundlessness of the nation's idealism. According to historian George Herring, the Vietnam War, like no other event in the nation's history, "challenged Americans' traditional beliefs about themselves, the notion that in their relations with other people they have generally acted with benevolence, the idea that nothing was beyond reach."[3]

Americans turned inward following Vietnam, fearful of any military engagements outside the defense of the continental United States, Alaska, and Hawaii. Polls taken in April 1975, just before the communists captured Saigon, indicated that only 36 percent of the American people felt that the United States should keep its commitments to other nations, and a mere 34 percent expressed a willingness to defend West Berlin should the Soviets try to take it by force. According to some polls, a majority of Americans would not rescue any country—other than Canada—from military attack if they were commander in chief.[4] For several years, then, the United States withdrew from international politics. For example, from the beginning of the Korean War in 1950 to the end of the Vietnam War in 1975, over one hundred thousand American soldiers lost their lives in combat. From 1975 until 2000, another twenty-five-year period, fewer than five thousand U.S. troops died in combat. Vietnam had indeed turned the nation off military intervention. Furthermore, the Vietnam War created a mood of despair in the United States. No one wanted to talk about Vietnam, and political leaders did not want to repeat it. It was impossible to put Vietnam to rest, however, and soon people were talking about a Vietnam syndrome, an unwillingness to engage the world out of fear of another Vietnam.

THE VIETNAM SYNDROME

The syndrome began even before the war ended. On April 22, 1975, President Gerald Ford told an audience at Tulane University that the Vietnam War was "finished as far as the United States was concerned."[5] One week later, on April 30, 1975, Saigon fell to combined PAVN and PLAF forces, and the U.S. war in Vietnam was indeed over. Hanoi moved quickly to consolidate power and unite Vietnam under the socialist banner. In Washington, the White House blamed Congress for refusing a request for $722 million in emergency military assistance for South Vietnam. Ford and his secretary of state,

Henry Kissinger, argued that additional aid might bring about the stalemate that all had hoped for in Vietnam and that would lead to a negotiated settlement between North and South Vietnam instead of an all-out communist victory. Kissinger publicly worried that "pulling the plug" on South Vietnam would have dire consequences for U.S. prestige in the world and that it would doom the South Vietnamese to "lingering deaths."[6] Congress, in sharp contrast, claimed that RVNAF troops had abandoned more military equipment in late 1974 and early 1975 than all the emergency aid could buy. Published photographs of RVNAF soldiers fleeing Phuoc Long, Hue, and Da Nang ahead of the communists did not endear Saigon's cause to Congress. It was time, Congress declared, to end U.S. involvement in this "horrid war."[7]

Following the fall of Saigon, U.S. policymakers dealt with the Vietnam syndrome in a variety of ways. Some, like Henry Kissinger, argued that the United States needed to abandon the reckless liberalism of the early cold war and focus more on its realistic national interests. Shortly after the war, Kissinger concluded that "we probably made a mistake" by focusing single-mindedly on international communism and falling dominos when dealing with Vietnam. "We perhaps might have perceived the war more in Vietnamese terms," he conceded, "rather than as the outward thrust of a global conspiracy."[8] In his view, the United States had stretched itself too thin in Vietnam and, in the future, must define its interests more narrowly. Like the European statesmen he had written about, Kissinger believed the true responsibility of a great power was in "knowing when to stop."[9] Kissinger recognized the United States could not fight a protracted war again and maintain its other, more vital interests. The

Soviet Union had reached nuclear parity while the United States was bogged down in the jungles of Southeast Asia, and it had also greatly expanded its naval fleet. Both developments changed the power relationship between the superpower rivals, and this change worried Kissinger more than the loss of South Vietnam.

Others tried to suggest that America could have won the Vietnam War and that the experience was no reason to limit U.S. global responsibilities. Nixon's secretary of defense, James Schlesinger, argued that the military had operated with too many restrictions. U.S. Army colonel Harry Summers agreed, advising that in the future the United States needed to bring all-out military force to bear in any conflict. General William Westmoreland believed that his attrition strategy could have worked in Vietnam if only the American people had not suffered a failure of will during the Tet Offensive. Some advisers suggested that the problem rested with the U.S. allies in Saigon. Without a viable government and a strong national army, how could the United States have achieved victory? McGeorge Bundy, national security adviser for Kennedy and Johnson, warned that Vietnam taught no useful lessons because the war was unique and probably not to be repeated. Americans, the Vietnam apologists all argued, should get over the war and turn their attention to the pressing international problems of the day.

But Congress still felt the limits on U.S. power following Vietnam. Six months after Saigon fell, Portugal granted its former colony, Angola, independence following a bloody civil war. The announcement set off another internal conflict involving the Soviet-supported Popular Movement for the Liberation of Angola (MPLA). The CIA spent $32 million on covert aid to the MPLA's rivals, hoping to control the revolution and events in Africa. The State Department official in charge of African affairs, Nathaniel Davis, urged the Ford administration to engage in trilateral diplomacy, bringing in neighboring Tanzania and Zambia to help negotiate a peaceful settlement. President Ford rejected Davis's advice, opting instead for more covert aid and a military solution. Davis resigned in protest and let several members of Congress know that the Ford administration had rejected the diplomatic path. As the MPLA made headway against its adversaries, Ford prepared to ask Congress for an additional $25 million for arms and covert aid. Congress balked, voting down the proposal by a wide margin. Kissinger immediately complained that Americans had been traumatized by Vietnam, and Ford concluded that Vietnam had caused members of Congress to "lose their guts."[10]

The Carter administration also experienced the hangover effect from Vietnam. Carter came to office in 1977 promising to cut military budgets, reduce U.S. forces overseas, trim arms sales abroad, and support allies who followed his human rights agenda. He vowed there would be "no more Vietnams." Carter was deeply troubled by the malaise that had gripped the nation since Vietnam. He believed the American people would no longer accept U.S. military intervention in faraway places for dubious reasons. He argued that the United States could not "prop up a series of regimes that lacked popular support," and that "there can be no going back to a time when we thought there could be American solutions to every problem."[11] Carter realized that newly emerging postcolonial nations were in revolt because of grinding poverty, social and racial problems, and political difficulties, not international communism. He wanted to reorient U.S. relations with the developing world, erasing the "intellectual and moral poverty" of military intervention that had been demonstrated in Vietnam.[12]

Yet Carter was also a cold warrior. He insisted that détente had allowed the Soviets to increase their domination of Eastern Europe, and he was highly critical of grain sales to Moscow. He reinvigorated the containment doctrine by initiating new weapons systems and by cultivating friendly governments in the Southern Hemisphere. When the Soviet Union invaded Afghanistan in 1979, Carter launched a new phase of containment. He armed many of Moscow's neighbors, such as Pakistan, and created several new naval facilities in Oman, Kenya, Somalia, and Egypt. Carter also opened formal diplomatic relations with the People's Republic of China, a move he was sure would make the Soviets think twice about more aggressive action. In his State of the Union address of January 23, 1980, the president announced the Carter Doctrine: "An attempt by any outside force to gain control of the Persian Gulf region will be regarded as an assault on the vital interests of the United States of America, and such an assault will be repelled by use of any means necessary, including military force."[13] Carter even declared a U.S. boycott of the 1980 summer Olympics in Moscow to protest the Soviet invasion of Afghanistan.

Carter's bold words caused many in Washington to proclaim that the Vietnam syndrome had already been cured. But others knew better. George F. Kennan, the father of the original containment policy, suggested that Carter was long on words and short on action. He concluded that the president was using "thundering" rhetoric but carrying "a very small stick."[14] Kennan knew what others knew. At the height of a devastating economic crisis at home, and in the shadow of Vietnam, Congress was not likely to approve of any bold plans that included direct military action against the Soviets. The United States could fight wars with proxies in the post-Vietnam era, but Congress would not go along with the full mobilization of U.S. troops to save Afghanistan—or any other nation in the region, for that matter. When Carter promised $400 million to Pakistan for its defense against a potential Soviet invasion, the Pakistani prime minister called it "peanuts."[15] Indeed, Carter was trying to fight the cold war with one hand tied behind his back. The knot was Vietnam. The hostage crisis in Iran in 1979 simply underscored Carter's inability to move the nation to a war footing so soon after the fall of Saigon.

Other signs indicated that Carter and the country were still suffering from the Vietnam syndrome. In 1975 the Khmer Rouge took over Cambodia following a brutal civil war against the American-backed Lon Nol government. The Khmer Rouge were not only Maoists but perhaps even more fanatical about the moral superiority of their ideas. Once they seized power, the communists emptied Phnom Penh and other Cambodian cities, creating a nation of refugees. They relocated the urban Cambodians to rural areas and forced them to work at meaningless tasks in death camps. Over time, the Khmer Rouge instituted one of the most reprehensible genocidal programs in history, killing over one-third of the entire Cambodian population. During this purge, the Carter administration sat on the sidelines. Of course, Washington's new relationship with Beijing made it difficult for the Carter administration to protest Khmer Rouge atrocities—China was the Khmer Rouge's major benefactor—but U.S. officials turned their backs, fearing another Vietnam. Carter purposefully avoided the genocide in Cambodia, according to John

Mueller, because of "fears that paying attention might lead to the conclusion that American troops should be sent over to rectify the disaster."[16] Carter was not alone in ignoring the problems in Cambodia. The three television networks devoted less than thirty minutes of coverage to a genocide that lasted over three years, and Congress failed to pass any resolutions condemning the Khmer Rouge and calling for united action by the U.S. foreign policy establishment and the United Nations..

Congress did go along with increased military budgets, however. If Carter could not deploy U.S. troops out of fear of another Vietnam, he definitely intended to beef up America's defense arsenal. The president deployed the MX intercontinental missile and added $47 billion in new weapons systems. The Pentagon's budget jumped from $170 billion in 1976 to $197 billion in 1981. Carter also doubled arms sales to U.S. allies between 1977 and 1980, to $15.3 billion.[17] Some critics suggested Carter was trying to "remilitarize" the United States, but others concluded he had been "too soft" on the Soviets and America's enemies.[18] His public opinion polls in the area of foreign affairs were some of the lowest of the twentieth century. Only 17 percent of Americans polled in 1980 gave the president a satisfactory rating.[19] For many Americans, Carter's mixed foreign-policy agenda only enforced the desire to isolate themselves from the rest of the world. In retrospect, Carter's problem was that he did not want to get involved in another Vietnam-type conflict, but the world held only more of the same. Afghanistan promised no easy solutions, and the civil wars in Central America were also open-ended commitments. Given the reluctance of Congress and the American people to repeat the Vietnam experience, the only avenue available to the president other than military intervention was to build up America's deterrent capabilities.

Carter could never balance U.S. fear of "more Vietnams" with broader foreign-policy objectives. His opponent in the 1980 presidential election found a solution to this foreign relations dilemma through tough cold-war rhetoric denying that Vietnam had been a defeat. Candidate Ronald Reagan claimed that policymakers in Washington had gotten Vietnam all wrong. "For far too long," Reagan declared in August 1980, "we have lived with the Vietnam Syndrome. This is a lesson for all of us in Vietnam. If we are forced to fight, we must have the means and the determination to prevail, or we will not have what it takes to secure peace. And while we are at it, let us tell those who fought in that war, that we will never again ask young men to fight and possibly die in a war our government is afraid to let them win."[20] Reagan was hoping to revise America's understanding of Vietnam and its meanings in order to pursue a more aggressive foreign-policy agenda. Carter's military budget increases paved the way for the Reagan administration to fight the cold war using new weapons and covert CIA operations.

THE WEINBERGER DOCTRINE

Despite Reagan's expansive rhetoric and expanded military budgets, however, his administration was the first to put parameters on U.S. military operations. In a speech before the National Press Club in November 1984, Reagan's secretary of defense, Casper Weinberger, announced the administration's new defense posture following the 1983 bombing of a U.S. Marine Corps barracks at the Beirut airport in Lebanon. That stunning terrorist act had caused the Reagan administration to withdraw all troops from Lebanon. The president did not want to isolate the United States from other overseas actions, but he did want the Defense Department to prepare a plan summarizing the lessons learned from Beirut and Vietnam. These lessons were distilled into six major points that became known as the Weinberger Doctrine:

- The United States should not commit forces to combat unless the vital national interest of the United States or its allies is involved.
- U.S. troops should be committed only wholeheartedly and with the clear intention of winning. Otherwise, troops should not be committed.
- U.S. combat troops should be committed to conflicts with clearly defined political and military objectives, with the capacity to accomplish those objectives.
- The relationship between the objectives and the force structure should be continually reassessed and adjusted if necessary.
- U.S. troops should be committed only when there is reasonable assurance that Congress and the American people will support the action.
- The use of arms should be the last resort to protect U.S. interests.

After the attack in Beirut and against the backdrop of Vietnam, Weinberger was limiting where and when the United States would engage in military intervention. Reagan's secretary of state, George Schultz, was a staunch critic of the Weinberger Doctrine, arguing that diplomacy needed the constant threat of military force to succeed. Schultz did not believe that the nation was suffering from any Vietnam syndrome, and he thought Congress would support U.S. military intervention whenever and wherever it was needed.

Given these parameters, the Reagan administration never asked the American people to make painful sacrifices to support its foreign policy agenda. Despite military intervention in several Central American countries, Reagan and Weinberger managed to keep U.S. military action quite limited on their watch. Few U.S. soldiers died in combat during the Reagan years, and there was no full-scale mobilization of the armed forces. Despite claims from many quarters that U.S. intervention in Nicaragua and El Salvador signaled new Vietnams, those conflicts resolved themselves in ways that proved the critics wrong. Reagan did not use the U.S. military to destabilize unfriendly regimes or to support friendly ones; instead, he used covert aid, CIA operations, and economic incentives to influence politics in the region. In Nicaragua and El Salvador, Reagan's support of authoritarian governments came more in the form of aid to proxy armies and death squads than direct U.S. military intervention. Even the administration's support of the contras in Nicaragua was limited militarily. The CIA helped the contras mine three Nicaraguan ports and built large bases in neighboring Honduras, but there was no full-scale use of U.S. forces against the Sandinistas.

The combination of the Beirut bombing and the lasting legacy of Vietnam indeed limited the president's use of force in undefined struggles. Instead of military intervention, the Reagan administration used America's unchallenged economic resources and covert operations to confront internal and external threats. The president increased military spending by 40 percent between 1980 and 1984, while cutting taxes. He believed he could outspend and outarm the Soviets with beneficial results. Reagan's flirtations with the Strategic Defense Initiative (SDI) were an outgrowth of that thinking. This missile shield was short on science but long on cost, and the Reagan administration believed that such a shield would force the Soviets into even more expensive weapon systems that did not significantly alter the strategic balance. The collapse of the Soviet Union was one sure sign that Reagan's policy of limiting U.S. military action abroad and focusing on a spiraling arms race had worked. However, that policy left the United States with record budget deficits, nearly $1 trillion, and a soaring balance-of-trade deficit. Still, most Americans felt confident about the nation's place in the world, and few feared the United States would be engaged in another Vietnam so soon after the collapse of South Vietnam.

THE POWELL DOCTRINE

After Reagan left office, many of his administration's views on military intervention survived with Colin Powell. Powell, a Vietnam veteran and a disciple of Casper Weinberger, maintained that the United States must continue to use its economic power, diplomatic skills, and multilateral support as the cornerstones of all foreign policy actions. He warned that the United States should never lead with the use of armed force. He said the country had to ask itself a series of questions before it actively engaged in military conflict:

- Is the political objective we seek to achieve important?
- Does it have a clearly defined objective that is easily understood?
- Have all other nonviolent policy means failed?
- Will military force achieve the objective?
- At what cost can the objective be reached?
- Have the gains and risks been analyzed?
- How might the situation that we seek to alter, once it is altered by force, develop further, and what might be the consequences?

In short, the Powell doctrine brought Weinberger's thinking into the 1990s.

Powell also outlined the military's willingness in the post-Vietnam era to ask hard questions and to make fundamental changes in its culture. Rejecting much of the academic thinking that had held sway during the cold war, the services returned to the basics. One of the first significant changes was introducing courses on strategy in the service academies.[21] These courses emphasized history over academic theory. Students studied the classic battles and investigated writers long ignored. Sun Tzu and Carl von Clausewitz became familiar names at West Point and Annapolis once again. Along with this renewed emphasis on military history and strategy came a belief among the officers that the principle lesson of the Vietnam War was that the United States should never find itself in that position again. The military began to concentrate again on the Soviet threat in Europe and to prepare for a more conventional war on the Continent. Military officers also came to reject many of the theories of protracted and

limited war as applied in Vietnam. Instead, those with Vietnam experience insisted that there were limits to U.S. power. They told their
troops that there was not always a military solution to complex political problems.

Another significant development to ensure no more Vietnams
was the move to make sure that service reserve troops were completely integrated into any mobilization scheme. During the Vietnam War, President Johnson had refused McNamara's request to
mobilize the reserves in 1965, fearing that the American public
would see such a move as a sure sign that the war would require
enormous sacrifice. Furthermore, Johnson wanted to limit public debate by fighting the war in cold blood. He worried that mobilizing
the reserves might spark a heated debate in Congress. Accordingly,
when Johnson introduced combat troops for the first time in March
1965, the reserves stayed home. It did not take long, however, for officers to complain to their commanders that without the reserves,
they presided over a depleted, unskilled, and demoralized army. The
lack of reserves also meant that many jobs usually given to support
troops went to the regular army, putting further pressure on force
structure. Even though Johnson routinely said that he had given
General Westmoreland everything he asked for, even abbreviated investigation would have revealed that officers in Vietnam rarely believed they had enough troops.

General Creighton Abrams, who served as U.S. Army chief of
staff in the last years of the Vietnam War, negotiated a new look for
the army with Secretary of Defense James Schlesinger. Abrams increased the army's size to sixteen divisions without increasing the
number of regular forces above 785,000.[22] He did so by assigning

most support functions to an expanded army reserve. The link with the regular army became so tight that Abrams guaranteed there could be no war without mobilizing the reserves. "They're not taking us to war again without calling up the reserves," Abrams was fond of saying.[23] The impact of this policy was felt immediately. Coupled with the Goldwater-Nichols Act of 1986, which gave the head of the Joint Chiefs of Staff greater responsibility over all service branches and allowed for coordinated and integrated training among the services, the new reserve-force structure meant the army would never be short of troops again. By the time of the first Gulf War, according to Herring, 70 percent of the army's support services, 60 percent of the air force's strategic airlift units, and 93 percent of the navy's cargo-handling battalions were with the reserves.[24] When the first President Bush took the nation to war in Iraq and Kuwait in 1991, he had no choice but to call up the reserves, and this arrangement made the president keep goals, objectives, and force structure in line.

Bush's mobilization for war followed Saddam Hussein's August 1990 invasion of Kuwait. After the Iraqi offensive in Kuwait, the Bush White House began making military plans for an air and ground offensive against Iraq should diplomacy fail. In late November, the Bush administration secured a UN resolution authorizing the use of force to expel the Iraqi army from Kuwait. In early January, Congress granted Bush the right to use force against the Iraqi army and to defend Saudi Arabia and Israel should Saddam Hussein launch attacks against them. The UN gave Baghdad a deadline of January 15, 1991, to withdraw from Kuwait, a time limit that Saddam Hussein ignored. Accordingly, on January 17, the allied attack against

Iraqi installations began. General Norman Schwarzkopf coordinated U.S. military action, combining air and ground attacks against key targets inside Iraq and Kuwait. In just six short weeks, allied military action had forced Saddam Hussein to beat a hasty retreat out of Kuwait and back to Baghdad. In the process, thousands of Iraqis were killed, and Iraqi military equipment worth millions was destroyed. The use of force had been overwhelming, and victory, decisive. President Bush, applauding the American-led effort, proclaimed, "By God, we've kicked the Vietnam syndrome."[25]

No, the Bush administration had not kicked the Vietnam syndrome. Instead, it had adopted a military strategy because of it. By massing overwhelming force for a very limited military objective, the administration was responding to nearly two decades of hard thinking on what had gone wrong in Vietnam. The force structure was commensurate with the job at hand, and the counterattacks against Iraq had the full support of Congress and the American people. Furthermore, the Bush administration had a UN resolution authorizing the action and several allies that went to battle alongside U.S. troops. Much of the Bush strategy rested on General Colin Powell's ideas on the use of military power. Bush did not march to Baghdad to force regime change. His administration, with the help of an international coalition, simply removed Saddam Hussein from Kuwait by force. In fact, the limited response to Iraq's aggressive action against Kuwait earned George H. W. Bush sharp criticism from many of those who would become his son's strongest supporters. They argued that the United States should have marched to Baghdad and thrown Saddam Hussein out of power then.[26]

Powell disagreed with the critics. He prophetically warned that to allow the United States to march to Baghdad was to ask for trouble. He opposed any U.S. military activity beyond the carefully prescribed UN resolution authorizing the use of force to expel Iraq from Kuwait. To do more, Powell insisted, was too great a risk. He explained in 1992 that if the first Gulf War had not been limited, "the United States would be ruling Baghdad today—at unpardonable expense in terms of money, lives lost and ruined regional relationships."[27] Powell also suggested that no military commander wanted to send his troops into harm's way without the full support of the American people and Congress. A march against Baghdad would surely have toppled Saddam Hussein, but then what? Powell did not want the country bogged down in a long-term nation-building project simply because it wanted regime change in Iraq. Like many of his fellow military leaders with Vietnam experience, Powell was cautious in the use of force. When it was applied, he wanted to have clear outcomes in mind and to use overwhelming force. The United States withdrew from the Iraqi theater with its limited objective met and its military ready for its next assignment.

The Ghosts of Vietnam

During the 1990s Balkan crisis, the Bush administration contemplated using force. When asked by a reporter if the United States would send troops to keep the peace among Bosnians, Serbs, and Croats, the president responded, "Everyone has been reluctant, for very understandable reasons, to use force. There are [sic] a lot of voices out there in the United States today that say 'use force,' but they don't have the same responsibility for sending somebody else's son or somebody else's daughter into harm's way. And I do. I do not want to see the United States bogged down in any way into some guerrilla warfare—we lived through that."[28]

Indeed, the Bosnian Serbs understood that the United States did not want to repeat Vietnam in the Balkans. Bosnian Serb leader Radovan Karadzic boldly proclaimed that his forces could have their way in the Balkans because the United States was paralyzed. He boasted the United States would have to send in two thousand marines to put down his forces, "then they have to send 10,000 more to save the 2,000. . . . This is the best way to have another Vietnam."[29] Another Serb leader claimed that the Balkans would be "a new Vietnam" if the United States sent in ground troops. According to Samantha Power, an expert on human rights and U.S. foreign policy, "'Vietnam' became the ubiquitous shorthand for all that could go wrong in the Balkans if the United States became militarily engaged."[30]

The ghosts of Vietnam also hampered the Clinton administration. Instead of immediately intervening in the Bosnian conflict, President Clinton publicly vowed that the United States would not send ground troops there, even to stop genocide. As *New York Times* journalist Drummond Ayres reported in May 1993, there was an "abiding fear that the Balkans are another Vietnam, a deep-seated angst that tends to outweigh concern that another holocaust is in the making."[31] This same fear kept the United States from intervening to stop the genocide in Rwanda. Instead of military intervention around the world, Clinton hoped to "engage" nations as the movement toward globalization and democracy transpired naturally. Clinton and his advisers believed that the president had to supervise this development by removing restrictions on trade and investment and the circulation of ideas. If this process could bind the nations of the world, the Clinton administration reasoned, the root causes of violence and interstate rivalry would fade away.[32] There would be no reason to repeat the mistakes of Vietnam because the fundamental underpinnings of conflict would have been destroyed. When the United States got bloodied in Somalia, Clinton quickly pulled the troops out and left that region of the world to fend for itself.

At the end of the 1990s, however, some foreign policy analysts claimed that the pressing international questions were no longer about fears of another Vietnam, but about ethical dilemmas concerning military intervention to support human rights. They asked how and when the United States and the United Nations should intervene to stop major human rights violations and genocide. Others suggested that the move toward capitalism and democracy was irreversible and that U.S. foreign policy should be aimed at helping that process along, not at seeking monsters to destroy.[33] Still, there was a growing feeling among many policy analysts that the Clinton administration was indeed suffering from the Vietnam syndrome. Its inability to "pull the trigger" in Rwanda to stop the genocide was a by-product of its worldview. Clinton's team players, most of them Vietnam-generation men and women, were hesitant to get involved in a complex situation that had elusive objectives and no easy answers. According to Samantha Power, Clinton administration officials were reluctant to get bogged down again, even if the cause was just.[34]

A major problem in fighting the Vietnam War was that the United States had suffered from challenges to its power for two decades. Defeat in Vietnam created a lasting feeling among many policymakers that they must avoid future Vietnams at all costs. The tragedy of Vietnam is that the misuse of force there limited U.S. military action where it might be required later. How does a country intervene in a messy situation like the Balkans or Rwanda after Vietnam? The Clinton administration never found a satisfactory answer until it was too late for tens of thousands of innocent people. One great lesson of Vietnam is that we must use power wisely. Another is that trouble will find a nation of America's power and responsibility without that nation's looking for it. At the end of a long day, intervening in Vietnam's civil war probably cost the United States many of its more important geopolitical objectives, including stopping intrastate violence and genocide.

NEOCONSERVATIVES REJECT THE VIETNAM SYNDROME

When George W. Bush decided to run for the presidency in 2000, he was certainly aware of the problems the Vietnam shadow had cast on the Clinton administration. During the campaign, Bush repeatedly voiced his concern about America's confused role in the world. He made traditional realist arguments about the limits on U.S. power, warning that the United States should not overextend its reach. He believed that the Clinton administration had pursued bad policy in the Balkans and in Africa, even if it had been limited. In the now-famous debate with Vice President Al Gore, candidate Bush stated that he did not believe U.S. troops should be used in lengthy nation-building exercises. The United States should use its power only when vital U.S. interests were at stake, Bush claimed. Taking a page from classic realism, Bush pledged that he would never follow the path of the reckless liberals who had taken the United States to war in Vietnam with no clear goal, no clear sense of purpose, and no plan to win.

Neoconservatives, who had helped elect Bush in 2000, were concerned, however, that the new president was acting too much like a "Henry Kissinger realist." Kissinger, they argued, had placed too much confidence in détente and too much stock in internationalism. He had emphasized that after the cold war, nations were free "to pursue foreign policies based increasingly on their immediate national interest." Furthermore, Kissinger argued, a new world order would emerge "much as it did in past centuries from a reconciliation and balancing of competing national interests."[35] Hoping to convince the president to accept their foreign policy agenda, the neocons urged the new president not to adopt a narrow view of U.S. national interests, as Kissinger had.[36]

Neoconservatives such as Paul Wolfowitz, William Kristol, and Lawrence Kaplan were right-wing Wilsonians who wanted to promote democracy around the world to strengthen it at home, a view in keeping with Woodrow Wilson's philosophy. They disagreed with Wilson's internationalism, however, favoring instead U.S. unilateral action outside an international framework. Neoconservatives believe that international institutions, such as the United Nations, limit the United States and keep it from achieving many of its foreign policy goals. Instead, they suggest, the United States has the legitimate right to pursue its own agenda because it exerts a benevolent hegemony.

Shortly before the second Iraq War, two leading neoconservatives, William Kristol and Robert Kagan, claimed that the world would accept U.S. efforts to promote democracy because the United States was inherently good and was perceived that way: "It is precisely because American foreign policy is infused with an unusually high degree of morality that other nations find they have less to fear from its otherwise daunting power."[37] Some neoconservatives, such as Max Boot, even suggested that a return to empire was neither unfeasible nor unrealistic. In his essay "The Case for an American Empire," Boot declared that the Untied States should provide troubled countries with enlightened administration, much as the British supposedly had during the Raj.[38]

After the terrorist attacks on September 11, 2001, President Bush pursued an aggressive policy against America's enemies in Afghanistan. On September 18, 2001, the UN Security Council passed a resolution demanding that the Taliban in Afghanistan hand over Osama bin Laden and close terrorist training camps inside the country's borders. The Taliban refused, arguing that the United States and its allies in the United Nations had no proof that bin Laden had been connected to the September 11 terrorist attacks, and that he should have his day in an Islamic court. The response was immediate and executed within a multilateral framework based on a United Nations resolution. On October 7, 2001, U.S. and British bombers attacked the Taliban in Kabul, Afghanistan's capital, and Kandahar, another Taliban stronghold. Ground troops followed, and soon an international coalition of eighteen nations was involved in the war on terrorism, including Japan, which for the first time since World War II was participating in military combat on a global scale. By December 2001, most of the Taliban had been defeated or had retreated to the mountains outside Tora Bora, the site of one of the last military engagements between the Taliban, the terrorists, and the international coalition. Although remnants of the Taliban and the al-Qaeda terrorist network continue to harass coalition troops, the Bush administration had struck a blow against terrorism with its swift and overwhelming response in Afghanistan.

In many ways, the attacks in Afghanistan followed the Powell Doctrine and the lessons of the Vietnam experience. The United States had gone to the UN for a Security Council resolution justifying the attacks inside an international framework. International support for the attacks was overwhelming, and public opinion around the world supported the United States in its hour of need. Perhaps at no time since the end of World War II had the United States enjoyed so much of the world's empathy. Bush used this international support wisely, building a coalition of willing allies to help the United States meet its limited objectives through the measured use of force. He also had the support of Congress, which passed a war powers resolution allowing President Bush to use the U.S. military against any force or any individual organization or state that had been involved in the attacks on September 11 or that sheltered, harbored, or assisted individuals involved in those attacks. Congress also passed a $40 billion appropriation bill to support the war on terrorism.

But something else happened in Afghanistan. Neoconservatives inside the Bush administration used the war on terror to push their larger agenda. They wanted to use U.S. power to promote democracy in the Middle East, and there is some evidence that this planning had been under way well before the September 11 attacks.[39] It now seems likely that the attacks on the United States by al-Qaeda convinced President Bush that the neoconservatives were right. Perhaps it was time to use American might benevolently to create a new world order. Like many U.S. policymakers before him, President Bush believed that the best defense against the terrorists was a good offense. The United States had the right to defend itself, the president claimed, but it also had a responsibility to make the world safe for democracy. As the world's only superpower, the United States had the power and the obligation to defend and promote democratic ideals. Leading neoconservatives William Kristol and Lawrence Kaplan agreed with the president, declaring that the United States was in the driver's seat and should drive the car: "What is wrong with dominance in the service of sound principles and high ideals?"[40]

According to historian John Gaddis, the Bush administration's response to the events of September 11 was to "undertake the most fundamental reassessment of American grand strategy in over half a century."[41] Bush's new grand strategy embraced much of the neoconservatives' thinking on democracy promotion, and he came to believe that regime change was essential in Iraq, and that promoting democracy through U.S. military power was the key to stopping future terrorist attacks. The United States had to extend peace through military intervention in a troubled region, according to this thinking. This view separated the Bush administration from its predecessors. Although President Reagan had talked of tearing down walls and promoting democracy, he had rarely involved U.S. troops. George H.W. Bush had used the military for a very limited objective and had purposefully ruled out regime change and democracy promotion through force. President Clinton had believed that peace would naturally happen, without America using its powerful military at all.

A NEW GRAND STRATEGY

George W. Bush's new grand strategy set out a policy line that denied that Vietnam had happened at all. Ironically, just as in Vietnam, the United States would use its considerable power to influence events in a country far away and for a people it knew little about, because key policymakers in Washington believed that such a policy would actually make Americans safer. Promoting democracy or anticommunism promised to rid the world of the conditions that had created threats to American ideals. The appeal to ideals is what separates the George W. Bush administration from other post-Vietnam administrations. Other presidents had talked about ideals, but few had built military intervention around them. Policymakers had indeed restricted the use of military force to solve complex political problems in the post-Vietnam era. In the Balkans, President Clinton had wanted to act early in the crisis but ultimately could not because he feared a long-drawn-out affair just like Vietnam. But President George W. Bush wanted to take the country on the offensive. The president's speech at West Point's graduation ceremonies in 2002 included these telling words: "We must take the battle to the enemy. . . . In the world we have entered the only path to safety is the path of action." Bush was clear about his moral certainty: "Moral truth is the same in every culture, in every time, and in every place. . . . We are in conflict between good and evil."[42] The appeal to American ideals did not go unnoticed by the cadets.

Shortly before the March 2003 invasion of Iraq, President Bush further distanced himself from the lessons of the Vietnam War by publicly proclaiming, "America's vital interests and our deepest beliefs are now one."[43] Attacking Iraq, the president claimed, was in U.S. national security interests, as was promoting democracy in the Middle East. Bush told the nation about U.S. war aims in clear and decisive language: "A liberated Iraq can show the power of freedom to transform that vital region. . . . Success in Iraq could also begin a new stage for Middle Eastern peace."[44] Wesley Clark, former commander of all coalition forces in Europe, worried that the Bush administration's "quasi-imperial vision" would create an "army of empire." In his book *Winning Modern Wars,* Clark warned that the Bush administration sought a new world order based on aggressive policy goals built on the back of a powerful military: "This was to be a new America, reborn from adversity and threat, reaching out constructively to the world, liberating peoples, reforming a vital region, enabling the emergence of a new, universal morality, and taking advantage of this unique window of American military dominance to secure into the foreseeable future our security and safety."[45] For Clark and others, this vision was all too grand. It required too much of the military, and its hubris was overwhelming.

Since the U.S. mission in Iraq began to bog down in April 2004, democracy promotion has come under fierce attack in the United States by liberals and conservatives. Furthermore, the Bush administration's base of support for the war in Iraq dried up, in the same way liberals had abandoned President Johnson. Now that the war in Iraq can be characterized instead as a nation-building experiment to promote democracy, former supporters of the war have turned against the administration. Even some neoconservatives no longer believe in the cause. Francis Fukuyama has rejected the notion that history can be pushed along by American power and will.[46]

AN IRAQ SYNDROME?

In 2008, the United States seems to have come full circle. Once again, it finds itself engaged in a war characterized by no clear boundaries, no clear exit strategy, no definition of victory, little allied support, no UN authority, rising costs, and public pressure to withdraw. The Bush administration learned nothing from the Vietnam War, and this mistake will haunt U.S. foreign policy for years to come. By promoting its revolutionary agenda, the Bush White House has actually limited future presidents in their range of options. The United States has already shown a reluctance to act more forcefully in dealing with several important crises. Iran was emboldened to pursue its nuclear objectives in part because the United States had already spent its bullets in Iraq. Surely, radicals around the globe understand that the Bush administration's recklessness in Iraq means that they now have a freer hand to act as long as they do not launch direct attacks against highly valued U.S. assets.

Furthermore, many in the foreign policy establishment have already complained that Congress and the American people are now insisting on multilateral action before the United States protects its interests overseas. Because of the foreign policy debacle in Iraq, Congress will expect a UN or NATO resolution before it votes in favor of hostile action. Such limitations are dangerous to U.S. foreign policy because many of America's allies have not supported needed intervention around the globe, even when it was in their own best interest. The crisis in Afghanistan is the perfect example of the trouble that now awaits the United States when its legitimate security interests are threatened but it has little help from allies. It would be ideal if U.S. interests could always have multilateral support, but history shows a great reluctance on the part of America's closest allies to engage the world directly. And by rejecting any role for the United Nations in Iraq, the United States has significant work to do to rebuild that relationship. Without UN support, U.S. foreign policy objectives are more difficult to achieve.

There is another danger in thinking there are no limits on American power: isolationist backlash. After five years of war in Iraq, a majority of Americans have withdrawn their support for most broadly defined U.S. foreign-policy objectives. America is gripped by a new isolationism that indicates a swing in public opinion away from internationalism. According to some experts, the percentage of Americans who believe that the United States "should mind its own business has never been higher since the end of the Vietnam war."[47] There already is an Iraq syndrome, one comparable to the Vietnam syndrome that forced that United States to take a hard look at its policies and practices. It seems likely that Congress will act in 2009 to limit the power of the new president and establish a timetable for an American withdrawal from Iraq. This is not how a nation with America's power and responsibilities should conduct its foreign affairs, by legislative fiat, but that is the price the United States will have to pay for the Bush administration's irresponsible policies in Iraq. This retrenchment could have dangerous consequences for the United States.

Fueling this isolationist impulse has been the failing U.S. economy. According to several leading economists, the war in Iraq will ultimately cost U.S. taxpayers an astonishing $2 trillion, and perhaps more.[48] In March 2008, the Joint Economic Committee, chaired by Senator Chuck Schumer (D-New York), held hearings on the war's costs. Several witnesses, including the Nobel Prize–winning economist Joseph Stiglitz, suggested that the cost to taxpayers could reach as much as $3 trillion if the war is not ended soon. Stiglitz argued that the money could have been put to better use elsewhere: "For a fraction of the cost of this war, we could have put Social Security on a sound footing for the next half-century."[49] Given the number of baby boomers about to start collecting Social Security, this sound footing would have been a beneficial strategy. Another leading economist, Robert Hormats, vice chairman of Goldman Sachs International, explained that the money spent in just one day in Iraq is enough to enroll an additional 58,000 children in Head Start for an entire year, or to give 160,000 low-income families a full Pell Grant for a year's college tuition.[50] And at no time in the nation's history has a president tried to fight a major war and cut taxes at the same time. The war in Iraq has also added about $2 trillion to the national debt. All of this has had a devastating effect on the nation's economy.

Lyndon Johnson used to say that he had brought that beautiful lady the Great Society to the ball but had spent all night dancing with that bitch Vietnam. Johnson sacrificed his dreams for a more tolerant and equitable America, one free of the misery of poverty, in the jungles of Vietnam. The neocons seem poised to suffer a similar fate. The Iraq War will set the aggressive neoconservative agenda back considerably. Furthermore, future policymakers will once again have trouble finding the appropriate balance between ideals and interests. Defending ideals is difficult when the American public wants to retreat from open-ended commitments that have ephemeral, even if noble, goals. One policy analyst believes that neoconservatism has become "indelibly associated with concepts like coercive regime change, unilateralism, and American hegemony."[51] If the Vietnam War killed cold war liberalism, the Iraq War could be the end of neoconservatism as a major political force in the United States.

U.S. policymakers went to war in Vietnam and Iraq with the expectation that a distinctively American story would emerge. It was not to be. One has to wonder if both wars were simply the miscalculations of a few shortsighted individuals, or if, in the words of cold war diplomat George Kennan, these wars reflect "a certain unfitness of the system as a whole for the conceiving and executing of ambitious political-military ventures far from our own shores."[52] In either case, it is time for the United States to reorient its power and begin to rebuild its relationships around the globe. This is not an easy process, but it is a necessary one. The next president will have to ask Americans to make painful sacrifices as the United States deals with the Iraq War fallout. Recovery could take years, but that long walk home has to start now.

ACKNOWLEDGMENTS

In writing this book, I have incurred many debts, both personal and intellectual. First on any list must be Deb Sharnak, my excellent research assistant, who provided a steady stream of material. I have also drawn a number of ideas from discussions with Frank Costigliola, Jeremi Suri, Mel Leffler, Richard Immerman, Mark Stoler, Walt LaFeber, Arne Westad, Mark Lawrence, Mark Lytle, Richard Aldous, Sandra Scanlon, Ann Heiss, Jack Langguth, Jim Blight, Janet Lang, Kyle Longley, Tom Blanton, Lloyd Gardner, Fred Logevall, David Elliot, Mai Elliot, Mark Bradley, David Anderson, David Ryan, Liam Kennedy, and Marilyn Young. Special help in the form of valuable comments on draft chapters came from my colleagues Steve Rock, Andy Davison, and Norma Torney; my former mentor, George C. Herring; and Charles Neu. Vietnam's senior foreign policy scholar, Luu Doan Huynh, shared his ideas with me at key junctures in this project. I am grateful to my colleagues in the History Department at Vassar College, who have provided such a supportive intellectual environment.

I owe special thanks to Fran Fergusson, Cappy Hill, Ron Sharp, Cathy Baer, and John Mihaly at Vassar, and to Bennett Boskey for his generous support of Vassar and me. The revisions for this paperback were done at University College Dublin while I was on a Fulbright. My colleagues in Ireland provided a warm and welcoming atmosphere. I am especially indebted to Peter Osnos, founder of PublicAffairs Books and now its editor-at-large, for his vision and faith in me. Peter is that rare publisher who loves books and ideas. My editor at PublicAffairs, Lindsay Jones, has been supportive of this project from the very beginning. Her good sense and keen mind have made this a better book. Thanks to Scott and Marion Morrison, Brian and Karyn Trapp, Bob and Louise Lynch, Christina Powers, Ray Schwartz, Ed Pittman, Chris Roellke, Bill Kay, and Jen Ippolito for pleasant diversions. I want to extend special thanks to my mother, my sister, and the rest of my extended family: the Brigham, Church, and Bradford clans. From the beginning to end of this project, my wife, Monica Church, has shared with me its frustrations and satisfactions. Her own creative and intellectual sensibilities inform many of these pages.

NOTES

Chapter One

1. Melvyn Leffler, "9/11 and American Foreign Policy," *Diplomatic History* 29 (June 2005): 395–413.

2. John Foster Dulles, "A Righteous Faith," *Life Magazine* 13 (December 28, 1952): 49–51. See also, Seth Jacobs, *America's Miracle Man in Vietnam: Ngo Dinh Diem; Religion, Race, and U.S. Intervention in Southeast Asia* (Durham, NC: Duke University Press, 2004), p. 74.

3. John F. Kennedy, "America's Stake in Vietnam," *Vital Speeches* 22 (August 1, 1956): 617–619.

4. George C. Herring, *America's Longest War: The United States and Vietnam, 1950–1975,* 4th ed. (New York: McGraw-Hill, 2002), p. 55.

5. Kennedy to Rusk and McNamara, November 14, 1961, Presidential Office Files, Box 128, John F. Kennedy Library, Boston, MA.

6. Jonathan Schell, *The Time of Illusion* (New York: Knopf, 1976), pp. 9–10.

7. Theodore C. Sorensen, ed., *Let the Word Go Forth: The Speeches, Statements, and Writings of John F. Kennedy, 1947–1963* (New York: Laurel, 1988), pp. 11–15.

8. Dean Rusk, *As I Saw It: A Secretary of State's Memoirs* (New York: I. B. Tauris, 1991), p. 413.

9. Kennedy to Rusk and McNamara, November 14, 1961, Presidential Office Files, Box 128, John F. Kennedy Library, Boston, MA.

10. *The Pentagon Papers*, Senator Gravel Edition, vol. 2 (Boston: Beacon Press, 1972), p. 111.

11. Fred Logevall, *Choosing War: The Lost Chance for Peace and the Escalation of War in Vietnam* (Berkeley: University of California Press, 1999), p. 31.

12. Thomas Paterson, "Bearing the Burden: A Critical Look at JFK's Foreign Policy," *Virginia Quarterly Review* 54 (Spring 1978): 197.

13. Robert E. Osgood, *Limited War: The Challenge to American Security* (Chicago: University of Chicago Press, 1957); Thomas Schelling, *Arms and Influence* (New Haven, CT: Yale University Press, 1966); and Herman Kahn, *On Escalation* (Baltimore: Penguin Books, 1965).

14. Thomas Schelling, *The Strategy of Conflict* (Cambridge, MA: Harvard University Press, 1960). See also Robert S. McNamara, James G. Blight, and Robert K. Brigham, *Argument Without End: In Search of Answers to the Vietnam Tragedy* (New York: PublicAffairs, 1999), p. 159.

15. McNamara et al., *Argument without End*, pp. 276–277.

16. Robert S. McNamara, *In Retrospect: The Tragedy and Lessons of Vietnam* (New York: Times Books, 1995), p. 277.

17. McNamara et al., *Argument Without End*, p. 412.

18. Bruce Palmer Jr., *The Twenty-Five Year War: America's Military Role in Vietnam* (Lexington: University of Kentucky Press, 1984), p. 177.

19. See Odd Arne Westad et al., eds., "77 Conversations between Chinese and Vietnamese Leaders on the Wars in Indochina, 1964–1977," Working Paper No. 22 of the Cold War International History Project (May 1998), Woodrow Wilson Center, Washington, DC.

20. Alan Whiting, *The Chinese Calculus of Deterrence* (Ann Arbor: University of Michigan Press, 1975), p. 176.

21. Guo Ming et al., *Zhongyue quanxi yanbian sishinian* [Forty-Year Evolution of Sino-Vietnamese Relations] (Nanking: Guangiz People's Press, 1992), p. 69.

22. Chen Jian, "China's Involvement in the Vietnam War, 1964–1969," *China Quarterly* 142 (June 1995): 373–375.

23. Philip Catton, *Diem's Final Failure: Prelude to America's War in Vietnam* (Lawrence: University Press of Kansas, 2002).

24. Robert Topmiller, *The Lotus Unleashed: The Buddhist Movement in South Vietnam, 1964–1966* (Lexington: University of Kentucky Press, 2002).

25. Contacts with Vietnamese Generals, October 23, 1963, Lyndon B. Johnson Papers, Box 2, Lyndon B. Johnson Library, Austin, TX.

26. Roger Hilsman, *To Move a Nation* (New York: Doubleday, 1967), p. 486.

27. Galbraith to Kennedy, April 4, 1962, Kennedy Papers, National Security File, Box 196, John F. Kennedy Library, Boston, MA.

28. *Resolution of Ninth Plenum*, Vietnam Documents and Research Notes, Document no. 19, U.S. Mission, Saigon. See also William Duiker, *The Communist Road to Power*, 2nd ed. (Boulder, CO: Westview Press, 1996), pp. 239–240.

29. Merle L. Pribbenow, *Victory in Vietnam: The Official History of the People's Army of Vietnam, 1954–1975* (Lawrence: University Press of Kansas, 2002), p. 124.

30. As quoted in Herring, *America's Longest War*, p. 113.

31. Memorandum of conversation at the White House, April 4, 1963, *Foreign Relations of the United States, Vietnam, 1961–1963*, vol. 3 (Washington, DC: Government Printing Office, 1991), pp. 198–200.

32. McNamara, *In Retrospect*, p. 96.

33. Taylor to Kennedy, November 3, 1961, in *Foreign Relations of the United States, Vietnam, 1961–1963*, vol. 1 (Washington: Government Printing Office, 1988), pp. 492–493.

34. Chester Cooper, *The Last Crusade* (New York: Dodd & Mead, 1972), p. 193.

35. McGeorge Bundy memorandum for the record, September 14, 1964, Johnson Papers, National Security File, Country File: Vietnam, Box 6, Lyndon B. Johnson Library, Austin, TX. See also, McNamara to Johnson, April 21, 1965, Johnson Papers, National Security File, Country File: Vietnam, Box 13, Lyndon Johnson Library, Austin, TX.

36. Herring, *America's Longest War*, p. 138.

37. As quoted in Larry Berman, *Planning a Tragedy: The Americanization of the War in Vietnam* (New York: W. W. Norton, 1982), p. 92.

38. The White House, Press Release, "U.S. Secretary of State Colin Powell Addresses the U.N. Security Council," February 5, 2003.

39. Ibid.

40. Ibid.

41. The White House, Press Release, "President Bush Outlines Iraqi Threat: Remarks by the President on Iraq," Cincinnati Museum Center-Cincinnati Union Terminal, Cincinnati, Ohio, October 7, 2002.

42. The White House, http://www.whitehouse.gov.

43. Ibid.

44. Ibid.

45. Elliot A. Cohen, *Supreme Command: Soldiers, Statesmen, and Leadership in Wartime* (New York: Free Press, 2002).

46. Richard Pipes, "Team B—The Reality behind the Myth," *Commentary* (October 1986): 25–40, and Murray Friedman, *The Neoconservative Revolution* (Cambridge: Cambridge University Press, 2005).

47. William Kristol and Robert Kagan, *Present Dangers* (San Francisco: Encounter Books, 2000), p. 20.

48. Bill Keller, "The Sunshine Warrior," *New York Times Magazine* (September 22, 2002): 50.

49. Ibid, pp. 51–52.

50. As quoted in David Elliott, "Parallel Wars? Can Lessons of Vietnam Be Applied to Iraq?" in Lloyd C. Gardner and Marilyn Young, eds., *Iraq and the Lessons of Vietnam* (New York: Free Press, 2007), p. 34.

51. Robert W. Tucker and David C. Hendrickson, *Empire of Liberty: The Statecraft of Thomas Jefferson* (New York: Oxford University Press, 1990).

52. Lloyd Gardner, *Safe for Democracy* (New York: Oxford University Press, 1984).

53. N. Gordan Levin Jr., *Woodrow Wilson and World Politics* (New York: Oxford University Press, 1968).

54. Background Information Relating to Southeast Asia and Vietnam, Committee Print, 90th Congress, 1st Session (Washington: Government Printing Office, 1967), pp. 148–153.

55. As quoted in Lloyd Gardner, *Pay Any Price: Lyndon Johnson and the Wars for Vietnam* (Chicago: Ivan R. Dee, 1995), p. 193.

56. Valenti Notes, Johns Hopkins Speech, Johnson Papers, Statements File, Box 143, Lyndon B. Johnson Library, Austin, TX.

57. Ibid.

58. As quoted in Stanley Karnow, *Vietnam: A History* (New York: Penguin Books, 1983), p. 419.

59. As quoted in Doris Kearns, *Lyndon Johnson and the American Dream* (New York: Harper & Row, 1976), p. 279.

60. Samuel Huntington, *The Clash of Civilizations and the Remaking of World Order* (New York: Simon & Schuster, 1996).

61. John Lewis Gaddis, *Surprise, Security, and the American Experience,* (Cambridge, MA: Harvard University Press, 2004), pp. 103–104.

62. As quoted in Gardner, *Pay Any Price,* p. 197.

63. Edwin Moise, *Tonkin Gulf and the Escalation of the Vietnam War* (Chapel Hill: University of North Carolina Press, 1996).

64. Eugene Windchy, *Tonkin Gulf* (New York: Doubleday, 1971), p. 24.

65. As quoted in Herring, *America's Longest War,* p. 142.

66. One influential study challenges these claims: Moise, *Tonkin Gulf,* pp. 142–155.

67. Summary Notes of the 538th Meeting of the National Security Council, August 4, 1964, Johnson Papers, National Security File, NSC Meeting File, Box 1, Lyndon B. Johnson Library, Austin, TX.

68. Chronology of Events, Tuesday, August 4 and Wednesday, August 5, 1964, Tonkin Gulf Strike, Johnson Papers, National Security File, Country File: Vietnam, Box 18, Lyndon B. Johnson Library, Austin, TX.

69. Herring, *America's Longest War,* pp. 143–144.

70. Ibid.

71. Chronology of Events, Tuesday, August 4, and Wednesday, August 5, 1964, Tonkin Gulf Strike, Johnson Papers, National Security File, Country File: Vietnam, Box 18, Lyndon B. Johnson Library, Austin, TX.

72. William Conrad Gibbons, *The U.S. Government and the Vietnam War: Executive and Legislative Roles and Relationships,* part 2 (Princeton, NJ: Princeton University Press, 1986), pp. 297–299.

73. As quoted in Gardner, *Pay Any Price,* p. 134.

74. As quoted in Gibbons, *The U.S. Government,* p. 297.

75. McNamara et al., *Argument without End,* pp. 23–24.

76. McNamara, *In Retrospect,* p. 163.

77. As quoted in Herring, *America's Longest War,* p. 144.

78. Ibid., p. 145.

79. As quoted in Anthony Austin, *The President's War* (Philadelphia: Lippincott, 1971), p. 98.

80. As quoted in Logevall, *Choosing War,* p. 203.

81. John Blum, *Years of Discord: American Politics and Society, 1961–1974* (New York: W. W. Norton, 1991), p. 232.

82. As quoted in Logevall, *Choosing War,* p. 205.

83. Herring, *America's Longest War,* p. 145.

84. White House Press Release, September 30, 2002.

85. White House Press Release, October 1, 2002.

86. Joint Resolution to Authorize the Use of United States Armed Forces in Iraq, White House Press Release, October 2, 2002.

87. Ibid.

88. "War Resolution," White House Press Release, October 16, 2002.

89. Ibid.

90. "Senate Approves Iraq War Resolution," CNN.com, October 11, 2002.

91. "State of the Union Address," White House Press Release, January 29, 2003.

92. Center for Cooperative Research, Press Release, February 20, 2003.

93. "Old Europe Hits Back at Rumsfeld," CNN.com, January 24, 2003.

94. Walter LaFeber, *The American Age: United States Foreign Policy at Home and Abroad since 1750* (New York: W. W. Norton, 1989), p. 59.

95. "Senate's Roll-Call Vote on King Holiday," *New York Times* (October 20, 1983), p. B9.

Chapter Two

1. U.S. Department of Defense, Office of the Assistant Secretary of Defense (Comptroller), Directorate of Information Operations, press release, March 19, 1974.

2. New Zealand Embassy, Washington, DC, Records of the New Zealand Ministry of External Relations and Trade, Wellington, New Zealand, press release, April 30, 1976.

3. Jeffrey Clarke, *Advice and Support: The U.S. Army in Vietnam; The Final Years, 1965–1973* (Washington, DC: Center for Military History, 1988), p. 461.

4. Pribbenow, *Victory in Vietnam*, pp. 80–84, 116, 156–157, 182, 191–192, 211, 339, 344–346, 356, 410, 464 fn. 14. See also Greg Lockhart, *Nation in Arms: The Origins of the People's Army of Vietnam* (Sydney, Australia: Allen & Unwin, 1989), p. 272.

5. Chen Jian, "China's Involvement in the Vietnam War, 1964–1969," *China Quarterly* 142 (June 1995): 373–375.

6. General Vo Nguyen Giap, *Tu Nhan dan ma Ra* [From the People] (Hanoi: Nha xuat ban su that, 1964).

7. Samuel P. Huntingon, "The Bases of Accommodation," *Foreign Affairs* 46 (July 1968): 652.

8. McGeorge Bundy to President Johnson, January 27, 1965, Memos to the President, Volume 8, January 1–February 28, 1965, Aides Files, McGeorge Bundy, Box 2, Lyndon B. Johnson Library, Austin, TX.

9. Logevall, *Choosing War*, p. 90.

10. George C. Herring, *LBJ and Vietnam: A Different Kind of War* (Austin: University of Texas Press, 1995), p. 23.

11. McNamara et al., *Argument without End*, pp. 176–177, 190–191, 193, 354.

12. William Westmoreland, *A Soldier Reports* (Garden City, NY: Doubleday, 1976), p. 168, 170–172, 194.

13. Clifford-Taylor Report, August 5, 1967, Johnson Papers, National Security File, Country File: Vietnam, Box 91, Lyndon B. Johnson Library, Austin, TX.

14. Herring, *America's Longest War*, p. 183.

15. John Prados, *The Blood Road: The Ho Chi Minh Trail and the Vietnam War* (New York: Wiley, 1999).

16. Critical Oral History Conference on the Vietnam War, June 1997, transcript, Watson Institute, Brown University, Providence, RI.

17. Ibid.

18. Herring, *America's Longest War*, p. 184.

19. Jeffrey Record and Andrew Terrill, *Iraq and Vietnam: Differences, Similarities, and Insights* (Carlisle, PA: Strategic Studies Institute, 2004), p. 10.; Mark Clodfelter, *The Limits of Air Power: The American Bombing of North Vietnam* (New York: Free Press, 1989), pp. 134, 166, 167, 194; and McNamara et al., *Argument without End*, p. 379.

20. Record and Terrill, p. 10; see also Clodfelter, *The Limits of Air Power*, p. 8.

21. McNamara et al., *Argument without End*, p. 342.

22. Ministry of Labor, War Invalids, and Social Affairs Press Release, Hanoi, Vietnam, April 4, 1995.

23. Clarke, *Advice and Support*, p. 275.

24. Ibid.

25. John Clay Thompson, *Operation Rolling Thunder* (Chapel Hill: University of North Carolina Press, 1980), and James William Gibson, *The Perfect War: The War We Couldn't Lose and How We Did* (New York: Vintage, 1986).

26. Malcom Browne, *The New Face of War* (Indianapolis, IN: Bobbs Merrill, 1968), p. ix.

27. William Colby, *Lost Victory: A Firsthand Account of America's Sixteen-Year Involvement in Vietnam* (Chicago: Contemporary Books, 1989), pp. 269–270, 319–320.

28. Melvin Laird, "Iraq: Learning the Lessons of Vietnam," *Foreign Affairs* (November/December 2005): 37.

29. Ibid., p. 26.

30. "COSVN Resolution Nine."

31. Matt Steinglass, "Vietnam and Victory," *Boston Globe* (December 18, 2005), pp. 3–4.

32. Ibid.

33. http://www.washingtonpost.com, Sunday, August 8, 1999.

34. Huntington, "The Bases of Accommodation," p. 653.

35. David Elliott, *The Vietnamese War: Revolution and Social Change in the Mekong Delta, 1930–1975*, vol. 2 (Armonk, NY: M. E. Sharpe, 2003), p. 1169.

36. Lewis Sorley, *A Better War: The Unexamined Victories and Final Tragedy of America's Last Years in Vietnam* (New York: Harcourt Brace, 1999).

37. Henry Kissinger, *Ending the Vietnam War* (New York: Simon & Schuster, 2003), pp. 115, 297–299.

38. Steinglass, "Vietnam and Victory," pp. 3–4.

39. Andrew Krepinevich, Jr., "How to Win in Iraq," *Foreign Affairs* 84 (September/October 2005): 91–93.

40. BBC News, at http://news.bbc.co.uk/1/hi/world/middle_east/737483.stm.

41. Krepinevich, "How to Win in Iraq," p. 87.

42. Peter Grier, "What a Troop Surge in Iraq Might Accomplish," *Christian Science Monitor* (December 26, 2006), p. 1.

43. Robert Kagan, "The Surge Is Succeeding," *Washington Post* (March 11, 2007), p. B7.

44. Ibid.

45. Thomas L. Friedman, "Remember Iraq," *New York Times* (October 24, 2007), p. 27.

46. Karl Mayer, "The Perfect Debacle," *World Policy Journal* 21 (Fall 2004): 102.

47. "A Conversation with Colin Powell," *The Atlantic Online* at http://www.the atlantic.com/doc/200408u/powell, August 2, 2004.

48. Le Duan, "Political Report to the Central Committee of the Lao Dong," in *The Third National Congress of the Vietnam Workers' Party: Documents*, vol. 1 (Hanoi: Foreign Languages Publishing House, 1961), p. 63.

49. Douglas Pike, *Viet Cong: The Organization and Techniques of the National Liberation Front of South Vietnam* (Cambridge, MA: Massachusetts Institute of Technology Press, 1966), pp. 92–93.

50. Ibid., p. 97.

51. Ibid., p. 115.

52. Jeffrey Race, *War Comes to Long An: Revolutionary Conflict in a Vietnamese Province* (Berkeley: University of California Press, 1972), p. 150.

53. For good descriptions of the Battle of Ap Bac, see Charles Neu, *America's Lost War* (Wheeling, IL: Harlan Davison, 2005), pp. 58–62; Herring, *America's Longest War*, p. 106; Karnow, *Vietnam*, pp. 259–262; Gabriel Kolko, *Anatomy of a War* (New York: Pantheon, 1985), pp. 146–147; Marilyn Young, *The Vietnam Wars* (New York: HarperCollins, 1991), pp. 89–90; and Neil Sheehan, *A Bright Shining Lie: John Paul Vann and America in Vietnam* (New York: Random House, 1988), pp. 198–199.

54. Hilsman, *To Move a Nation*, pp. 442–456.

55. Ibid., p. 432.

56. See Robert K. Brigham, "Why the South Won the American War in Vietnam," in Marc Gilbert, ed., *Why the North Won the Vietnam War* (New York: Palgrave, 2002), p. 103. See also, Duiker, *The Communist Road*, pp. 215–239.

57. Philippe Devillers, "The Struggle for Unification in Vietnam," *China Quarterly* 9 (January/March 1962): 2–23.

58. U.S. Department of State, "A Threat to Peace: North Vietnam's Effort to Conquer South Vietnam," December 1961, Document No. 00358, Douglas Pike Collection, NLF Documents, Indochina Archive, University of California at Berkeley.

59. McNamara et al., *Argument without End*, p. 321.

60. *U.S.-Vietnam Relations, 1945–1967*, 12 vols., prepared by the U.S. Department of Defense and printed by the House Committee on Armed Services, Washington, DC, 1971, Reference is to vol. 2, section IV.A.5., p. 2.

61. "The Vietnam Workers' Party's 1963 Decision to Escalate the War in the South," *Viet-Nam Documents and Research Notes*, U.S. Mission, Saigon, Document No. 96, July 1971.

62. Nguyen van Hieu, *Ban be ta khap nam chau* [Our Friends around the World] (Hanoi: Nha Xuat Ban Van Hoc, 1963).

63. The NLF's Ten Point Program can be found in translation at http://vietnam.vassar.edu/docnlf.html.

64. For a critical description of this belief, see Steven Metz, "Insurgency and Counterinsurgency in Iraq," *Washington Quarterly* 27 (Winter 2003–2004): 26–29.

Chapter Three

1. Transcript of presidential debates, Commission on Presidential Debates, online at http://www.debates.org/pages/trans2000a.html.

2. Lawrence Freedman, "Writings of Wrongs," *Foreign Affairs* 85 (January/February 2006): 132.

3. Paul Pillar, "Intelligence, Policy, and the War in Iraq," *Foreign Affairs* 85 (March/April 2006): 16.

4. "Turf Wars and the Future of Iraq," *Frontline* online at http://www.pbs.org/wgbh/pages/frontline/shows/truth/fighting/turfwars.html.

5. Ibid.

6. Ibid.

7. Ibid.

8. Ibid.

9. Rand Corporation, *America's Role in Nation-Building: From Germany to Iraq* (Santa Monica, CA, March 2003).

10. Dominique Vidal, "A Guide to Nation-building," *Le Monde diplomatique* (December 2003): 1.

11. Rand, *America's Role,* p. xxvii.

12. Ibid.

13. See Douglas Porch, "Review, James Dobbins' *America's Role in Nation-Building: From Germany to Iraq*," *Strategic Insights* 3 (February 2004): 14.

14. Benedict Anderson, *Imagined Communities: Reflections on the Origin and Spread of Nationalism* (London: Verso, 1991).

15. Eric Hobsbawm, *Nations and Nationalism since 1780: Programme, Myth, and Reality* (Cambridge: Cambridge University Press, 1990), and Eric Hobsbawm and Terence Ranger, *The Invention of Tradition* (Cambridge: Cambridge University Press, 1983).

16. Ernest Renan, "What Is a Nation?" trans. and annotated Martin Thom, in Geoff Eley and Renald Grigor Suny, eds., *Becoming National: A Reader* (New York: Oxford University Press, 1996), p. 52.

17. Michael Howard, *The Lessons of History* (New Haven, CT: Yale University Press, 1991), p. 2.

18. Barbara Ehrenreich, *Blood Rites: Origins and History of the Passions of War* (New York: Henry Holt, 1997), p. 200.

19. Niall Ferguson, "Op-Ed," *New York Times* (April 18, 2004), p. A43.

20. Interview with Nguyen Co Thach, former Foreign Minister, Socialist Republic of Vietnam, Hanoi, Vietnam, June 1997.

21. *May van de tong ket chien tranh va viet lich su quan su* [Selected Issues Related to the Conclusions and the Writing of the Military History of the War] (Hanoi: Nha xuat ban su that, 1987); Pham van Dong, "Phat huy chu nghia anh hung cach mang, day manh su nghiep chong My, cuu nuoc den thang loi hoan toan" [Promote Revolutionary Heroism, Strengthen the Anti-U.S. Resistance War for National Salvation of the Fatherland to Lead to Complete Victory], *Hoc Tap* 13 (January 1967): 17–20; and Robert K. Brigham, "Revolutionary Heroism and Politics in Postwar Vietnam," in Charles Neu, ed., *After Vietnam: Legacies of a Lost War* (Baltimore: Johns Hopkins University Press, 2000), pp. 85–104.

22. Frances FitzGerald, *Fire in the Lake: The Vietnamese and the Americans in Vietnam* (New York: Vintage, 1972), p. 512.

23. William Duiker, *Vietnam: Revolution in Transition*, 2nd ed. (Boulder, CO: Westview Press, 1995), p. 123.

24. Ronald Spector, *Advice and Support: The Early Years of the U.S. Army in Vietnam, 1941–1960* (New York: Free Press, 1985), p. 237.

25. Record and Terrill, *Iraq and Vietnam*, p. 45.

26. Anthony Cordesman, *The Iraq War: Strategy, Tactics, and Military Lessons* (Washington, DC: Center for Strategic and International Studies, 2002), p. 554. See also Jeffrey Record, *Dark Victory: America's Second War with Iraq* (Annapolis, MD: Naval Institute Press, 2003), pp. 141–142.

27. Stephen Biddle, "Seeing Baghdad, Thinking Saigon," *Foreign Affairs* 85 (March/April 2006): 8.

28. Ibid., p. 9.

29. John F. Burns and Alissa J. Rubin, "U.S. Arming Sunnis in Iraq to Battle Old al-Qaeda Allies," *New York Times* (June 11, 2007), p. A1.

30. Ibid.

31. Clarke, *Advice and Support*, pp. 161–163.

32. General Duong van Khuyen, *RVNAF* (Washington, DC: Center for Military History, 1988), pp. 181–182.

33. Laird, "Iraq: Learning the Lessons," p. 29.

34. "President Richard Nixon's Speech to the Nation on Vietnam, November 3, 1969," *Public Papers of President Richard Nixon, 1969* (Washington, DC: Government Printing Office, 1970), p. 431.

35. Political Transcript Wire, Lanham, MD, December 2, 2005, Wire Feed.

36. White House Press Release, President Bush Speech before VFW, January 10, 2006.

37. Ibid.

38. "General Says Training of Iraqi Troops Suffered from Poor Planning and Staffing," *New York Times* (February 11, 2006), p. A6.

39. Ibid.

40. Ibid.

41. Ibid.

42. *The Pentagon Papers: The Secret History of the Vietnam War, as published by the New York Times* (New York: Bantam Books, 1971), p. 420.

43. Deployment of Forces, Saigon to Washington, June 5, 1965, National Security File, NSC History, Box 4, Lyndon B. Johnson Library, Austin, TX.

44. *The Pentagon Papers*, pp. 419–420.

45. General William Westmoreland, *Report on Operations in South Vietnam, January 1964–June 1968* (Washington, DC: Government Printing Office, 1969), p. 109.

46. Herring, *America's Longest War*, p. 166–167.

47. David S. Cloud and Michael R. Gordon, "Buildup in Iraq Needed into '08, U.S. General Says," *New York Times* (March 8, 2007), p. 14.

48. Clarke, *Advice and Support*, p. 463.

49. Ibid., p. 503.

50. Ibid.

51. General Duong van Khuyen, *RVNAF.*

52. Central Intelligence Agency, *World Fact Book on Iraq* (Washington, DC: Government Printing Office, 2005).

53. Ibid.

54. Ibid.

55. Bob Herbert, "The Destroyers," *New York Times* (February 13, 2006), p. A23.

56. Ibid.

57. Biddle, "Seeing Baghdad," p. 8.

58. Ibid.

59. Eric Schmitt, "Iraq-Bound Marine Leaders Cram on Civics and Economics," *New York Times* (February 13, 2006), p. A8.

60. "Elections in Iraq," *Washington Post* (December 15, 2005), p. A32.

61. Walt Rostow, *The Process of Economic Growth* (New York: W. W. Norton, 1952).

62. Ibid.

63. Laird, "Iraq: Learning the Lessons of Vietnam," p. 35.

64. Tran van Don, *Our Endless War inside Vietnam* (San Rafael, CA: Presidio Press, 1978), p. 241.

65. Duong Van Mai Elliot, *The Sacred Willow* (New York: Oxford University Press, 1999), p. 385. See also Malcom Browne, "Deep Recession Grips Saigon," *New York Times* (June 4, 1972), p. A1.

66. Sabrina Tavernise, "As Iraqi Shiites Police Sunnis, Rough Justice Feeds Bitterness," *New York Times* (February 6, 2006), p. A1.

67. Ibid.

68. John Mueller, "The Iraq Syndrome," *Foreign Affairs* 84 (November/December 2005): 50.

69. Fareed Zakaria, *The Future of Freedom: Illiberal Democracy at Home and Abroad* (New York: W. W. Norton, 2003).

70. Ibid.

71. Adam Przeworski, "The Poor and the Viability of Democracy," in Anirudh Krishna, ed., *Poverty, Participation, and Democracy* (New York: Cambridge University Press, 2008).

Chapter Four

1. Gardner, *Pay Any Price,* p. 297.

2. Mueller, "The Iraq Syndrome," p. 44.

3. Ibid.

4. Hazel Erskine, "The Polls: Is War a Mistake?" *Public Opinion Quarterly 34* (Spring 1970): 134–150.

5. Pew Research Center for the People and the Press, *The Public Struggles with Possible War in Iraq,* January 30, 2003.

6. Susan Page, "Poll: American Attitudes on Iraq Similar to Vietnam Era," *USA Today* (November 15, 2005), p. 1.

7. *Gallup Poll: Public Opinion 1935–1971,* 3 vols. (New York: Random House, 1972); 1972–1977 and later volumes (Wilmington, DE: Scholarly Resources).

8. Mueller, "The Iraq Syndrome," p. 45.

9. Ibid.

10. As quoted in Mueller, "The Iraq Syndrome," p. 45.

11. Ibid.

12. "The War in Vietnam," Draft No. 1, Johnson Papers, Statement File, Box 143, Lyndon B. Johnson Library, Austin, TX.

13. Ibid.

14. "Second Draft, March 20, 1968," Johnson Papers, NSC Histories, Box 128, Lyndon B. Johnson Library, Austin, TX.

15. Ibid.

16. As quoted in Richard Stebbins, *The United States in World Affairs, 1967* (New York: Published for the Council on Foreign Relations by Simon & Schuster, 1968), p. 68.

17. Herring, *America's Longest War*, pp. 220–221.

18. Walt Rostow to Ellsworth Bunker, September 27, 1967, Johnson Papers, DSDUF, Box 4, Lyndon B. Johnson Library, Austin, TX.

19. Depuy to Westmoreland, October 19, 1967, William Depuy Papers, Folder WXYZ–67, U.S. Army Military History Institute, Carlisle Barricks, PA.

20. *Tet Mau Than 68* [Tet 1968] (Hanoi: Ban Tuyen Huan Trung Uong, 1988).

21. Louis Harris, *The Anguish of Change* (New York: W. W. Norton, 1973), pp. 63–64. See also Burns Roper, "What Public Opinion Polls Said," in Peter Braestrup, ed., *Big Story: How the American Press and Television Reported and Interpreted the Crisis of Tet in 1968 in Vietnam and Washington* (New Haven, CT: Yale University Press, 1983), pp. 674–704.

22. As quoted in Don Oberdorfer, *Tet!* (Garden City, NY: Doubleday, 1971), p. 158.

23. Robert Elegant, "How to Lose a War," *Encounter 57* (August 1981): 73–90.

24. As reported in Jay Rosen, "The News from Iraq Is Not Too Negative: But It Is Too Narrow," *Pressthink* (May 26, 2004), p. 2.

25. Michael Massing, "Now They Tell Us," *New York Review of Books* 51 (February 26, 2004): 34–35.

26. After Action Report by the Senior Advisor, Seventh Infantry Division, January 9, 1963, JCS Files, Center for Military History, Washington, DC. See also, Karnow, *Vietnam*, p. 262.

27. William Prochnau, *Once upon a Distant War: David Halberstam, Neil Sheehan, Peter Arnett; Young War Correspondents and Their Early Vietnam Battles* (New York: Times Books, 1995), p. 232.

28. Ibid., p. 235.

29. Neil Sheehan, "Costly Vietnam Battle Angers U.S. Advisers," *Washington Post* (January 3, 1963), p. 1.

30. Neil Sheehan, "Vietnamese Ignored U.S. Battle Order," *Washington Post* (January 7, 1963), p. 1. For a reprint of the article, see *Reporting Vietnam* (New York: Library of America, 1998), pp. 68–70.

31. David Halberstam, "Vietcong Downs Five U.S. Copters, Hits Nine Others," *New York Times* (January 3, 1963), p. 1.

32. David Halberstam, "Vietnamese Reds Win Major Clash," *New York Times* (January 4, 1963), p. 2.

33. David Halberstam, "Vietnam Defeat Shocks U.S. Aides," *New York Times* (January 6, 1963), p. 2.

34. See *Reporting Vietnam*, pp. 68–70.

35. Prochnau, *Once upon a Distant War*, p. 239.

36. Ibid., p. 240.

37. *Foreign Relations of the United States, Vietnam, 1961–1963: January–August 1963*, vol. 3 (Washington, DC: Government Printing Office, 1991), p. 3.

38. David Halberstam, *The Making of a Quagmire* (New York: Random House, 1965), p. 158.

39. Interestingly, many authors suggest that Felt's comments were directed at others, not Malcom Browne. Stanley Karnow suggests the remark was meant for Peter Arnett of the Associated Press; see Karnow, *Vietnam*, pp. 260–262. John Clarke Pratt argues that Felt directed his response to Neil Sheehan of United Press International; see John Clarke Pratt, *Vietnam Voices* (New York: Penguin, 1984), pp. 126–127. And Prochnau claims that Browne was indeed the intended recipient of Felt's anger.

40. Critical Oral History Conference on the Vietnam War, June 1997, transcript, Watson Institute, Brown University.

41. As quoted in Karnow, *Vietnam*, p. 487.

42. *Gallup Poll: Public Opinion 1935–1971*, vol. 3 (New York: Random House, 1972).

43. *Public Papers of the President, Richard M. Nixon, 1969* (Washington, DC: Government Printing Office, 1971), pp. 901–909.

44. Ibid.

45. Charles Babington, "Hawkish Democrat Joins Call for Pullout," *Washington Post* (November 18, 2005), p. A1.

46. As quoted in John Mulligan, "Historians, Soldiers Hesitant to Call Iraq Another Vietnam," *Providence Journal* (April 25, 2004), p. A8.

47. Ibid.

48. Ibid.

49. Bartholomew Sullivan, "The Road from Tet to Fallujah," *Commercial Appeal* (May 30, 2004), p. B3.

50. Susan Page, "Is Iraq Becoming Another Vietnam," *USA Today* (April 14, 2004), p. 1A.

51. Bob Herbert, "Powell, Then and Now," *New York Times* (September 27, 2004), p. A27.

52. Robert Kuttner, "Exit Iraq," *Washington Post* (November 7, 2004), p. B7.

53. Lawrence Freedman, "Rumsfeld's Legacy: The Iraq Syndrome?" *Washington Post* (January 9, 2005), p. B5.

54. Babington, "Hawkish Democrat Joins Call," p. A1.

55. Ibid.

56. "Cheney Calls War Critics 'Opportunists,'" MSNBC News Service, 9:00 am, November 17, 2005.

57. Babington, "Hawkish Democrat Joins Call," p. A1.

58. Jonathan Rauch, "Iraq Is No Vietnam, but Vietnam Holds Lessons for Iraq," *National Journal* 36 (September 11, 2004): 2710–2711.

59. Anthony Zinni, "Making Vietnam's Mistakes All Over Again," *New Perspectives Quarterly* 21 (Summer 2004): 24–28.

60. Barbara Slavin, "McCain: Force Levels in Iraq Inadequate," *USA Today* (November 5, 2003), p. A1.

61. Ibid.

62. Gary Jacobson, a political scientist at the University of California at San Diego, has studied this partisan divide. See Michael Fletcher, "Iraq Critics Meet Familiar Reply; White House Reverts to Blistering Attacks of 2004 Campaign," *Washington Post* (November 18, 2005), p. A6.

63. Ibid.

64. Quoted in Thomas Powers, *Vietnam: The War at Home* (New York: Grossman, 1973), p. 118.

65. Melvin Small, *Johnson, Nixon, and the Doves* (New Brunswick, NJ: Rutgers University Press, 1988), p. 60.

66. Sidney Verba, et al., "Public Opinion and the War in Vietnam," *American Political Science Review* 61 (June 1967): 317–333, and Peter Sperlich and William Lunch, "American Public Opinion and the War in Vietnam," *Western Political Quarterly* 32 (March 1979): 21–44.

67. Critical Oral History Conference on the Vietnam War, June 1997, transcript, Watson Institute, Brown University.

68. Charles DeBenedetti, *An American Ordeal: The Antiwar Movement of the Vietnam Era* (Syracuse, NY: Syracuse University Press, 1990), pp. 203–204.

69. Rowland Evans and Robert Novak, "Johnson's Home Front," *Washington Post* (July 30, 1965), p. 1.

70. Notes on Meeting with Congressional Leadership, January 25, 1966, Johnson Papers, Meeting Notes File, Box 1, Lyndon Johnson Library, Austin, TX.

71. Herring, *America's Longest War*, p. 278.

72. Carl Huse and Jeff Zeleny, "Democrats Fail to Force Vote on Iraq Pullout," *Washington Post* (July 18, 2007), p. 1.

73. "General Petraeus Testifies before Congress on the Status of Iraq," *Congressional Quarterly Wire* (September 10, 2007).

74. Ibid.

75. Karen DeYoung and Tom Ricks, "Report Finds Little Progress on Iraq Goals," *Washington Post* (August 30, 2007), p. A1.

76. http://www.foreignaffairs.house.gov/110/lantos091007.htm.

77. Critical Oral History Conference on the Vietnam War, June 1997, transcript, Watson Institute, Brown University.

78. Logevall, *Choosing War*, pp. 272–273.

79. Memorandum from the Secretary of State to the President, January 8, 1964, *Foreign Relations of the United States, Vietnam, 1964–1968*, vol. 1 (Washington, DC: Government Printing Office, 1992), pp. 9–10.

80. Logevall, *Choosing War*, p. 373.

81. Critical Oral History Conference on the Vietnam War, February 1998, transcript, Watson Institute, Brown University.

82. As quoted in Gardner, *Pay Any Price*, p. 315.

83. As quoted in Kearns, *Lyndon Johnson and the American Dream*, pp. 263–265, 272.

84. Herring, *America's Longest War*, p. 136.

85. As quoted in ibid, p. 136.

86. Brian VanDeMark, *Into the Quagmire* (New York: Oxford University Press, 1990), pp. xv, 60.

87. Michael Beschloss, *Taking Charge: The Johnson White House Tapes* (New York: Simon & Schuster, 1998), 403.

88. Herring, *America's Longest War*, p. 138.

89. McNamara et al., *Argument without End*, p. 292.

90. *The Pentagon Papers: United States–Vietnam Relations, 1945–1967; Study Presented by the Department of Defense,* vol. 6 (Washington, DC: Government Printing Office, 1971), pp. 124–125.

91. McNamara, *In Retrospect,* p. 286.

92. Herring, *America's Longest War,* p. 215.

93. McNamara, *In Retrospect,* p. 307.

94. Richard Helms, Memorandum for the President, September 12, 1967, Country File: Vietnam, National Security Files, Box 259/260, Lyndon B. Johnson Library, Austin, TX.

95. Laird, "Iraq: Learning the Lessons of Vietnam," p. 27.

96. As reported in Steve Grove, "The Question on the Corner," *Boston Globe* (May 2, 2004), p. 1.

97. China, Dr. Kissinger's Visit, June 1972 Memcons Folder, National Security Council Kissinger Office Files, Box 97, and Polo I, Kissinger Briefing Book, July 1971 Trip to China, National Security Council, Box 850, Nixon Presidential Materials Project, National Archives and Records Administration, College Park, MD.

98. As quoted in Jussi Hanhimaki, *The Flawed Architect: Henry Kissinger and American Foreign Policy* (New York: Oxford University Press, 2004), p. 225.

99. Memorandum of Conversation, June 20, 1972, 2:05–6:06pm, Great Hall of the People, China: Dr. Kissinger's Visit, June 1972 Memcons Folder, National Security Council, Kissinger Office Files, Box 97, Nixon Presidential Materials Project, National Archives and Records Administration, College Park, MD.

100. Ibid.

101. Ibid.

102. Conversation 760–766, August 3, 1972, 8:28–8:57am, Oval Office, Nixon Presidential Materials Project, National Archives and Records Administration, College Park, MD.

103. Luu van Loi and Nguyen Anh Vu, *Tiep xuc bi mat Viet Nam-Hoa Ky truoc hoi nghi Pa-ri* [Secret Contacts between Vietnam and the United States before the Paris Talks] (Hanoi: Vien Quan He Quoc Te, 1990), pp. 188–191.

104. Critical Oral History Conference on the Vietnam War, February 1998, transcript, Watson Institute, Brown University.

105. As quoted in Karnow, *Vietnam*, p. 636.

106. http://www.senate.gov/~levin/newsroom/release.cfm.

107. *Iraq Study Group Report*, December 2006, p. 6.

108. Herring, *America's Longest War*, pp. 246–247.

109. Acheson to John Cowles, March 14, 1968, Dean Acheson Papers, Yale University Library, Box 7, New Haven, CT.

110. Terry Anderson, *The Movement and the Sixties: Protest in America from Greensboro to Wounded Knee* (New York: Oxford University Press, 1995), pp. 178–179.

Chapter Five

1. Francis Fukuyama, "After Neoconservatism," *New York Times Magazine* (February 19, 2006), p. 65.

2. "An Irony of History," *Newsweek* (April 28, 1975), p. 17.

3. Herring, *America's Longest War*, p. 346.

4. Ibid., p. 349.

5. "President Gerald R. Ford's Address at a Tulane University Convocation, April 23, 1975," at http://www.ford.utexas.edu/LIBRARY/speeches/.750208.htm.

6. Notes on Cabinet Meeting, April 16, 1975, Ron Nessen Papers, Box 294; Memorandum of Conversation, Kissinger, Ford, and Congressional Leaders, March 5, 1975, Kissinger/Scowcroft File, Box A1, Gerald Ford Library, Ann Arbor, MI.

7. *Congressional Record*, 94th Congress, 1st Session, pp. 10101–10108.

8. Quoted in Neu, *America's Lost War*, p. 225.

9. Paul Kennedy, *The Rise and Fall of the Great Powers* (New York: Random House, 1987), p. 408.

10. Quoted in Thomas Franck and Edward Weisband, *Foreign Policy by Congress* (New York: Oxford University Press, 1979), p. 46.

11. Quoted in "Vance Would Put Controls on U.S. Covert Operations," by Murray Morder, *Washington Post* (January 12, 1977), p. 1.

12. *Public Papers of the President, Jimmy Carter,* vol. 1(Washington, DC: Government Printing Office, 1977), p. 197.

13. *Department of State Bulletin*, 80 (February 1980): Special B.
14. As quoted in Thomas Paterson et al., *American Foreign Policy*, 3rd ed. (Lexington, MA: D. C. Heath, 1991), p. 641.
15. Quoted in Gaddis Smith, *Morality, Reason, and Power* (New York: Hill & Wang, 1986), p. 232.
16. Mueller, "The Iraq Syndrome," p. 53.
17. LaFeber, *The American Age*, pp. 665–666.
18. Smith, *Morality, Reason, and Power*, pp. 9, 81–84.
19. LaFeber, *The American Age*, p. 666.
20. Neu, *America's Lost War*, p. 227.
21. Edward Coffman, "The Course of Military History in the United States since World War II," *Journal of Military History* 61 (October 1997): 769–770.
22. George Herring, "Preparing Not to Refight the Last War: The Impact of the Vietnam War on the U.S. Military," in Charles Neu, ed., *After Vietnam: Legacies of a Lost War* (Baltimore: Johns Hopkins University Press, 2000), p. 65.
23. Lewis Sorley, *Thunderbolt: General Creighton Abrams and the Army of His Times* (New York: Simon & Schuster, 1992), pp. 360–365.
24. Herring, "Preparing Not to Refight," p. 65.
25. Quoted in Neu, *America's Lost War*, p. 229.
26. Cohen, *Supreme Command*.
27. Colin Powell, "U.S. Forces: Challenges Ahead," *Foreign Affairs* 71 (Winter 1992–1993): 37.
28. "News Conference with President Bush," Federal News Service, August 7, 1992.
29. As quoted in Samantha Power, *A Problem from Hell: America and the Age of Genocide* (New York: Perennial, 2002), p. 284.
30. Ibid.
31. B. Drummond Ayres, "In American Voices, a Sense of Concern over Bosnia Role," *New York Times* (May 2, 1993), p. 4.
32. Gaddis, *Surprise, Security*, pp. 77–78.
33. Francis Fukuyama, *The End of History and the Last Man* (New York: Free Press, 1992).

34. Power, *A Problem from Hell*, pp. 283–285, 294, 315.

35. Henry Kissinger, *Diplomacy* (New York: Simon & Schuster, 1994), p. 803.

36. William Kristol and Lawrence Kaplan, *The War over Iraq* (San Francisco: Encounter Books, 2003), p. 47.

37. As quoted in Fukuyama, "After Neoconservatism," p. 66.

38. Max Boot, "The Case for an American Empire," *Weekly Standard* (October 15, 2001), p. 2. See also Max Boot, *The Savage Wars for Peace: Small Wars and the Rise of American Power* (New York: Basic Books, 2002), and Niall Ferguson, *Colossus: The Price of America's Empire* (New York: Penguin Books, 2004).

39. Richard Clarke, *Against All Enemies: Inside America's War on Terror* (New York: Free Press, 2004).

40. Kristol and Kaplan, *The War over Iraq*, p. 112.

41. Gaddis, *Surprise, Security*, p. 81.

42. As quoted in Wesley Clark, *Winning Modern Wars: Iraq, Terrorism, and the American Empire* (New York: PublicAffairs, 2003), p. 163.

43. Second Bush Inaugural Address, White House Press Release, January 19, 2005.

44. Clark, *Winning Modern Wars*, p. 164.

45. Ibid.

46. Fukuyama, "After Neoconservatism," p. 65.

47. Ibid., p. 63.

48. Bob Herbert, "The $2 Trillion Nightmare," *New York Times* (March 4, 2008), p. A37.

49. Ibid.

50. Ibid.

51. Fukuyama, "After Neoconservatism," p. 67.

52. George F. Kennan, *The Cloud of Danger: Current Realities of American Foreign Policy* (Boston: Little Brown, 1977), pp. 4–5.

INDEX

Robert K. Brigham is the Shirley Ecker Boskey Professor of History and International Relations at Vassar College. He is the author of numerous books and essays on American foreign relations, including *Argument Without End: In Search of Answers to the Vietnam Tragedy* written with Robert S. McNamara and James G. Blight.

PublicAffairs is a publishing house founded in 1997. It is a tribute to the standards, values, and flair of three persons who have served as mentors to countless reporters, writers, editors, and book people of all kinds, including me.

I.F. Stone, proprietor of *I. F. Stone's Weekly*, combined a commitment to the First Amendment with entrepreneurial zeal and reporting skill and became one of the great independent journalists in American history. At the age of eighty, Izzy published *The Trial of Socrates*, which was a national bestseller. He wrote the book after he taught himself ancient Greek.

Benjamin C. Bradlee was for nearly thirty years the charismatic editorial leader of *The Washington Post*. It was Ben who gave the *Post* the range and courage to pursue such historic issues as Watergate. He supported his reporters with a tenacity that made them fearless and it is no accident that so many became authors of influential, best-selling books.

Robert L. Bernstein, the chief executive of Random House for more than a quarter century, guided one of the nation's premier publishing houses. Bob was personally responsible for many books of political dissent and argument that challenged tyranny around the globe. He is also the founder and longtime chair of Human Rights Watch, one of the most respected human rights organizations in the world.

. . .

For fifty years, the banner of Public Affairs Press was carried by its owner Morris B. Schnapper, who published Gandhi, Nasser, Toynbee, Truman, and about 1,500 other authors. In 1983, Schnapper was described by *The Washington Post* as "a redoubtable gadfly." His legacy will endure in the books to come.

Peter Osnos, *Founder and Editor-at-Large*